THE
DECIPHERMENT OF
LINEAR B

Canto is a new imprint offering a range of titles,
classic and more recent, across a broad spectrum of
subject areas and interests. History, literature,
biography, archaeology, politics, religion,
psychology, philosophy and science are all
represented in Canto's specially selected list of
titles, which now offers some of the best and most
accessible of Cambridge publishing to a wider
readership.

Michael Ventris

THE
DECIPHERMENT OF
LINEAR B

BY

JOHN CHADWICK

*formerly Reader in the Greek Language in the University of Cambridge,
and Honorary Fellow, Downing College
Fellow of the British Academy*

SECOND EDITION

CAMBRIDGE
UNIVERSITY PRESS

Published by the Press Syndicate of the University of Cambridge
The Pitt Building, Trumpington Street, Cambridge CB2 1RP
40 West 20th Street, New York, NY 10011–4211, USA
10 Stamford Road, Oakleigh, Victoria 3166, Australia

Library of Congress Catalogue Card Number 67-26066

First Edition 1958
Reprinted 1959
Reprinted with corrections and a Postscript 1960
Second Edition 1967
Reprinted 1970, 1976, 1979, 1982, 1984, 1987
Canto Edition 1990
Reprinted with a new Postscript 1992

Printed in Great Britain by
Billing & Sons Ltd, Worcester

ISBN 521 39830 4 paperback

CONTENTS

ILLUSTRATIONS

PLATES

FIGURES

PREFACE

The decipherment of Linear B was described by Michael Ventris in the first two chapters of our joint book, *Documents in Mycenaean Greek* (Cambridge University Press, 1956). This is an attempt to present that story to the general reader, so it omits many of the technical details to be found there; on the other hand, the vital steps in the decipherment are here explained in more detail, and much of the background which is unfamiliar to the general reader is filled in. In particular I have, by the kindness of Mrs Ventris, been able to make use of letters, notes, and other material from Ventris' files. My own file of letters between us, at times two or three a week, has been the chief source for the history of the subject after the first break in 1952. This has allowed me to round out the bare account by the inclusion of personal reminiscences and other details, much indeed that but for the tragic accident of Ventris' death would probably have remained unpublished; for his overwhelming modesty would have prevented me from writing the eulogy which I, and all his colleagues in this field, feel is his due. I had, however, his permission and encouragement to write a book on this subject; I hope it will be a worthy tribute to his memory.

Readers who are familiar with Greek, and even some who are not, may feel inclined to pursue the subject further. I have not provided them with the customary guide to further reading for two reasons: first because their next step has already been hinted at—they must read *Documents in Mycenaean Greek*, which contains a large bibliography up to 1955. Secondly, I find it impossible to select from the current mass of literature sufficient articles, especially in English, which are not either brief summaries of what is already in this book or technical studies of abstruse points. We have not yet reached the point where any more general surveys have been attempted, or at least have succeeded. Those who wish to make themselves familiar with the formidable volume of articles will find an index to it in *Studies in Mycenaean Inscriptions and Dialect*, started in 1955 by Ventris, and continued by L. R. Palmer and myself, and published by the London University Institute of Classical Studies. Another useful bibliography, covering work on all aspects of the Mycenaean world, is Miss B. Moon's *Mycenaean Civilization, Publications since 1935* (London, 1957, published by the same Institute).

Then a word to my professional colleagues: this book is not for them, though I hope they will enjoy reading it. I have tried to summarize the story as I see it, and have deliberately omitted much that I know is relevant, much that deserves a place in an official history. I hope no one will take me to task for failing to mention *X*'s contribution or *Y*'s theory; some parts are already hard work for the reader, and I have no wish to add to them. Chapter 7, though based upon chapter 5 of *Documents*, is my selection from the numerous views on Mycenaean life which have been expressed in the last few years; it was impossible to avoid some controversial topics, and the views expressed are my own responsibility. But I have drawn heavily on the publications of others, and I should like to take this opportunity of acknowledging my indebtedness to all whose work I have used, whether their names are mentioned or not.

It is a pleasure to record my thanks to the many friends and colleagues who have contributed advice and criticism, especially Mr O. Cox, Dr A. P. Treweek, and Professor T. B. L. Webster; and to the officers and staff of the University Press, who have devoted much time and care to the book. My thanks are also due to the Syndics of the Press for undertaking the publication, and for permitting me to use figures and plates prepared for *Documents*.

Above all I am grateful to Mrs Ventris, who has not only allowed me to consult her husband's papers, but has given me valuable help and encouragement at every stage.

J. C.

CAMBRIDGE
December 1957

01		da	30	ni	59	ta
02		ro	31	sa	60	ra
03		pa	32	qo	61	o
04		te	33	ra_3	62	pte
05		to	34		63	
06		na	35		64	
07		di	36	jo	65	ju
08		a	37	ti	66	ta_2
09		se	38	e	67	ki
10		u	39	pi	68	ro_2
11		po	40	wi	69	tu
12		so	41	si	70	ko
13		me	42	wo	71	dwe
14		do	43	ai	72	pe
15		mo	44	ke	73	mi
16		pa_2	45	de	74	ze
17		za	46	je	75	we
18			47		76	ra_2
19			48	nwa	77	ka
20		zo	49		78	qe
21		qi	50	pu	79	zu
22			51	du	80	ma
23		mu	52	no	81	ku
24		ne	53	ri	82	
25		a_2	54	wa	83	
26		ru	55	nu	84	
27		re	56	$pà_3$	85	
28		i	57	ja	86	
29		pu_2	58	su	87	

Chart of eighty-seven Linear B signs, with numeral equivalents and
phonetic values.

CHAPTER I

MICHAEL VENTRIS

The urge to discover secrets is deeply ingrained in human nature;
even the least curious mind is roused by the promise of sharing
knowledge withheld from others. Some are fortunate enough to
find a job which consists in the solution of mysteries, whether it
be the physicist who tracks down a hitherto unknown nuclear
particle or the policeman who detects a criminal. But most of us
are driven to sublimate this urge by the solving of artificial puzzles
devised for our entertainment. Detective stories or crossword
puzzles cater for the majority; the solution of secret codes may be
the hobby of a few. This is the story of the solving of a genuine
mystery which had baffled experts for half a century.

In 1936 a fourteen-year-old schoolboy was among a party who
visited Burlington House in London to see an exhibition organized
to mark the fiftieth anniversary of the British School of Archaeology at Athens. They heard a lecture by the grand old man of
Greek archaeology, Sir Arthur Evans; he told them of his discovery of a long forgotten civilization in the Greek island of Crete,
and of the mysterious writing used by this fabulous people of pre-
history. In that hour a seed was planted that was dramatically to
bear fruit sixteen years later; for this boy was already keenly
interested in ancient scripts and languages. At the age of seven he
had bought and studied a German book on the Egyptian hieroglyphs. He vowed then and there to take up the challenge of the
undeciphered Cretan writing; he began to read the books on it,
he even started a correspondence with the experts. And in the
fullness of time he succeeded where they had failed. His name
was Michael Ventris.

As this book is largely the story of his achievement, it will not
be out of place to begin with a short account of his life. He was

I

born on 12 July 1922 of a well-to-do English family, which came originally from Cambridgeshire. His father was an Army officer in India, his mother a highly gifted and beautiful lady who was half-Polish; she brought him up in an artistic atmosphere, and accustomed him to spend his holidays abroad or in visiting the British Museum. His schooling too was unconventional; he went to school at Gstaad in Switzerland, where he was taught in French and German. Not content with this, he quickly mastered the local Swiss-German dialect—an accomplishment that later on endeared him at once to the Swiss scholars whom he met—and even taught himself Polish when he was six. He never outgrew this love of languages; a few weeks in Sweden after the war were enough for him to become proficient in Swedish and get a temporary job on the strength of it. Later he corresponded with Swedish scholars in their own language. He had not only a remarkable visual memory, but, what is rarely combined with it, the ability to learn a language by ear.

Back in England, he won a scholarship to Stowe School, where, as he once told me with typical modesty, he 'did a bit of Greek'. One cannot help thinking that his unusual interests would have made him difficult to fit into a normal school routine; but he seems to have settled down happily enough, though none would then have prophesied that his hobby would make him famous. He did not go on to a university; he had made up his mind to become an architect, and he went straight to the Architectural Association School in London. The war came to interrupt his studies, and he enrolled in the R.A.F., where he flew as navigator in a bomber squadron. Characteristically he chose navigation. 'It's so much more interesting than mere flying', he remarked; and on one occasion he horrified the captain of his aircraft by navigating solely by maps he had made himself.

After the war, he returned to the study of architecture, and took his diploma with honours in 1948. Those who saw his work as a student were impressed and predicted a brilliant future for him as

2

an architect. He worked for a time with a team at the Ministry of Education engaged on the design of new schools; and he and his wife, herself an architect, designed a charming modern house for themselves and their two children. In 1956 he was awarded the first *Architects' Journal* Research Fellowship; his subject was 'Information for the Architect'.

He might well have become one of the leading figures in his profession; but it was not in this way that he was to win fame. He had never lost his interest in the Minoan scripts, and with a rare concentration he devoted much of his spare time to painstaking studies of that abstruse problem. In 1952 he claimed to have found the key to its understanding, a claim which has been fully vindicated during the last five years. Honours he received included the Order of the British Empire 'for services to Mycenaean palaeography', the title of honorary research associate at University College, London, and an honorary doctorate of philosophy from the University of Uppsala. These were but a foretaste of the honours that would surely have been paid to him.

'Those whom the gods love die young', said the Greek poet Menander; yet we had never dreamed that the life which had shown so much genius, and held promise of so much more, would be cut short in the very hour of triumph. On 6 September 1956, when he was driving home alone late at night on the Great North Road near Hatfield, his car collided with a lorry, and he was killed instantly.

For me, who had the privilege of being his friend and of working closely with him for more than four years, it is hard to find words in which to describe him. I know how he would recoil from extravagant praise; yet he was a man whom nothing but superlatives fitted. His brilliance is witnessed by his achievement; but I cannot do justice to his personal charm, his gaiety and his modesty. From the beginning he advanced his claims with suitable caution and hesitancy; a promising sign to those who had repeatedly experienced the assurance of previous decipherers. But even when his success was assured, when others heaped lavish praise on him, he remained simple and unassuming, always ready to listen, to help and to understand.

If we ask what were the special qualities that made possible his achievement, we can point to his capacity for infinite pains, his powers of concentration, his meticulous accuracy, his beautiful draughtsmanship. All these were necessary; but there was much more that is hard to define. His brain worked with astonishing rapidity, so that he could think out all the implications of a suggestion almost before it was out of your mouth. He had a keen appreciation of the realities of a situation; the Mycenaeans were to him no vague abstractions, but living people whose thoughts he could penetrate. He himself laid stress on the visual approach to the problem; he made himself so familiar with the visual aspect of the texts that large sections were imprinted on his mind simply as visual patterns, long before the decipherment gave them meaning. But a merely photographic memory was not enough, and it was here that his architectural training came to his aid. The architect's eye sees in a building not a mere façade, a jumble of ornamental and structural features; it looks beneath the appearance and distinguishes the significant parts of the pattern, the structural elements and framework of the building. So too Ventris was able to discern among the bewildering variety of the mysterious signs, patterns and regularities which betrayed the underlying structure. It is this quality, the power of seeing order in apparent confusion, that has marked the work of all great men.

CHAPTER 2

THE MINOAN SCRIPTS

The year 776 B.C. witnessed the first Olympic games, a festival which all the Greeks kept at the precinct of Zeus at Olympia in the north-west of the Peloponnese. Whether it was really the first is doubtful, but it was so reckoned by the later Greeks whose records went back to that date. It is a significant date in Greek history because it marks and symbolizes the adoption in Greece of the Phoenician alphabet, from which ultimately all other alphabets are descended; from the eighth century B.C. onwards the Greeks were a literate people, able to record their own history. Thus Greek history in the strict sense may be said to begin then, and what lies before that date can be termed pre-history. But this was no more the beginning of Greek history than A.D. 1066 was of British. Long before that men and women had lived, fought and died among the mountains and islands of Greece, and by the only test which can properly be applied, that of language, they were as Greek as their successors.

There are three ways of penetrating the fog which blots out the early stages of the development of the Greeks; none of them satisfactory or offering more than scraps of information, but by a cautious synthesis allowing some general conclusions.

First, there is the memory of people and events which survived into a literate era. The Greeks of the classical period had many legends of a remote past, a heroic age when men were capable of heroic feats and the gods were always at hand to help; many of the heroes were the sons of gods or goddesses. There are two notable events recorded in these legends: the war against Thebes in Boeotia and the expedition against Troy. The latter is better known, since it provides the background for the twin masterpieces of Greek literature, the *Iliad* and the *Odyssey*. These, traditionally the work of Homer, are long epic poems which seem to have acquired their present form somewhere towards the end of the eighth century B.C.—again that significant century, when writing changed much of the Greek way of life, not least its poetry.

Poets there must have been before Homer, but nothing of their works remains—or so we thought. But modern research has shown that Homer was not a brilliant imaginative artist who created his poems out of his head. He not only made use of an existing legend; we now believe that he was in fact the last, and greatest, of a long line of epic poets who had sung the tale of Troy. Sung, not written; for the process of composition is quite different among illiterate peoples from what we know to-day. The bard, if we may borrow a Celtic word to translate the Greek *aoidos*, 'singer', was called upon to entertain the company with stories of heroic deeds; and he recited his tale using stock turns of phrase, well-known formulas and epithets, but each time improvising afresh on the basic theme. In this way we can surmise that the legends Homer used, including quite trivial details, had been transmitted from an earlier age. The impossibility of reconstructing real history from such material is obvious. The legends recorded after Homer are legion, but they are inconsistent and it is hopeless to try to sift out the few grains of truth they probably contain. Much in the Homeric tale too is clearly due to the imagination of the bards. But here at least is a strong pointer to a period of Greek pre-history when the country was organized in strong kingdoms centring round Mycenae—though in historical times this was no more than a small country town.

It was real enough to persuade a romantically minded German business man of the nineteenth century, Heinrich Schliemann, to retire from business and devote his time and wealth to the pursuit of tangible evidence of this forgotten age. Thus was forged the second tool of the Greek prehistorian, archaeology. Digging for buried treasure was already becoming elevated into a rudimentary science, and the aim was no longer the mere discovery of precious or curious articles. With the amateur's faith and enthusiasm Schliemann set out, Homer in hand, to bring to light the god-built walls of Troy.

This is not the place to record his career in detail; but we must pause for a moment to recall his momentous excavation of 1876, when he found the famous grave circle at Mycenae. For it was the revelation of the wealth and artistry of the civilization he unearthed that convinced scholars of the essential truth behind the legends. 'Mycenae rich in gold', sang Homer; and the gold came from the shaft graves in quantities to stagger even Schliemann. It took many years of patient work by Schliemann's successors to establish the pattern of events which can now be traced in outline. Pre-Hellenic archaeology, as it has been called until the last few years, distinguishes three phases of the Bronze Age in Greece: Early Bronze, roughly 2800–1900 B.C.; Middle Bronze, 1900–1600 B.C.; Late Bronze, 1600–1100 B.C. The great flowering of civilization took place first in Crete in the Middle period, culminating in a violent destruction about 1400 B.C. On the mainland it took place rather later, beginning with the Late Bronze Age and lasting until the twelfth century, when one after another all the important centres of Greece were sacked and left in ruins. It is this last period which is called, after the first site to be excavated and its chief centre, Mycenaean.

Among the many scholars who were in Athens in the 1890's to see the Schliemann treasures was an English scholar named Arthur Evans. His appreciation of the high level of civilization reached by these Mycenaeans led him to speculate on the economic structure of a kingdom wealthy enough to produce such art and monuments. Mycenae has no natural wealth—no gold or silver mines, or any other exploitable commodity. Yet the craftsmanship of her products implied intense specialization, and this in turn an economic system in which the means of life were available to specialized workers. Did not this demand a system of writing which should serve at least for the book-keeping of the palace secretariat? Evans thought for this and similar reasons that the Mycenaeans must have been able to write; but no inscriptions had been found in their graves and palaces; and the Greek alphabet was generally considered to have been borrowed from Phoenicia two or three hundred years after the fall of Mycenae.

It was this speculation that spurred Evans to search for traces of prehistoric writing; and his attention was attracted by some engraved gems which could be found in the antique-dealers' shops in Athens. They showed a style of composition clearly different from those known in the Near East, and some had arbitrary collocations of signs which might represent a kind of script. Evans traced these to Crete, and while the island was still under Turkish rule and in a state of ferment, he traversed it from end to end with another young man, who was later to share with him the honour of a knighthood, John Myres. They found abundant evidence of the origin of these seal-stones, for they were frequently worn by peasant women as charms; the women called them 'milk-stones'. From their study Evans first identified the earliest script of Greece.

But this was not enough. A few characters engraved on gems were no evidence of the book-keeping needed to run a civilized country. He determined to dig himself, and in 1900, as soon as the liberation of Crete from Turkish rule opened the way, he began the excavation of a site already well known as that of Knossos, a classical town of importance and, if Homer could be trusted, the royal seat and capital of a legendary empire. His first object, the discovery of writing, was rapidly accomplished; the first tablets were found on 30 March, only a week after he had started to dig. But as he went on, season after season, clearing the complex of buildings which he had unearthed, the excitement of that discovery was forgotten in a new theory which grew in his active mind. Civilization in Crete was incomparably older than in Greece; and even in the Late Bronze Age it was still more advanced. Legend told of Athens' subjection to King Minos of Crete; here was the alien civilization which held the Greeks in

thrall. Legend told of the tribute of maidens and youths sent
annually to satisfy the monster of the labyrinth; rationalization
demanded that the labyrinth should be only a vast and complex
palace, the monster Minos, the cruel monarch. So was born the
theory of an un-Greek Cretan civilization, named from its
legendary ruler, Minoan. The similarities between its art and

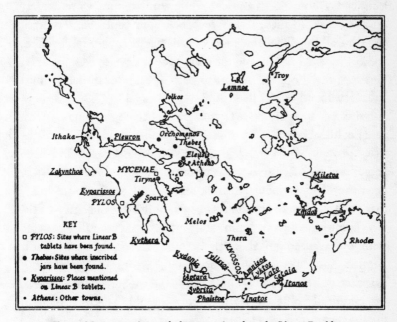

Fig. 1. Mycenaean sites, and places mentioned on the Linear B tablets.

architecture and those of mainland Greece were easily explained
if Greece was a Minoan province; and the rise of Mycenae could
be imagined as the revolt of a colony, which ended by destroying
and dominating the mother city.

The third clue was even more difficult to follow correctly, and
even today it is all too often overlooked: it is the study of the
Greek language. When the earliest alphabetic inscriptions were
made, in the eighth century B.C., every little state had its own
dialect. It is as if each English county had its own form, not only

9

of spoken, but of written language. But all the Greeks could, more or less, make themselves understood throughout the country; the local dialects were all fragments of one language, split up into pockets by the mountains and the sea. These dialects could, however, be grouped into four main divisions, though these do not correspond to their geographical distribution. Quite unlike dialects had a common frontier, while similar ones were widely separated. From these facts two conclusions could be drawn: at one time all these Hellenic peoples had ancestors who spoke alike; their unity was broken, and the main groups developed separately. Finally, just before the historical period, each local dialect must have developed out of its group.

Now we can apply these facts to the archaeological picture with some confidence. It used to be thought that at least three of the main groups of dialects had evolved outside Greece and been brought in by successive waves of invaders. This theory has lately been modified by new research, and it now seems more likely that the break-up of the dialects began only after the entry of the Greeks into the Balkan peninsula. This has been plausibly equated with the archaeological break between the Early and Middle Bronze Age cultures, about 1900 B.C. At most sites there is evidence of destruction at this period, and the new culture shows some radically different features from the old. The final stage of the movements of the Hellenic peoples is even better defined. The chief areas of Mycenaean power, the sites of the palaces destroyed about the thirteenth to twelfth centuries, were in historical times occupied by one of the major linguistic groups, the Dorians. Starting from north-west Greece (Epirus), these dialects lay in a great arc running down the west coast of the Peloponnese, through Crete, and up to Rhodes and Cos in the Dodecanese. Inside the arc, the Dorians penetrated central Greece as far as Delphi, and absorbed the whole of the Peloponnese except its mountainous core, Arcadia, which remained a separate linguistic enclave. But they never penetrated to the islands of the central

Aegean, or to the east coast of the mainland north of the Isthmus. This, combined with legends about the Dorian conquest, makes it extremely probable that it was this movement that caused the final collapse of Mycenaean power; though the possibility must still be considered that the collapse was due to some external force, and that the Dorians simply moved into a political vacuum.

Fig. 2. Greek dialects about 400 B.C.

Linguistically therefore there was good reason to regard the Mycenaeans as Greeks, as Schliemann had done. The experts, however, were more cautious, and a variety of theories of their origin were current. In the light of the decipherment these can now be set aside; but we must remember them in order to appreciate the views current up to 1952. What was especially significant about the dialects was that the isolated dialect of the central Peloponnese, Arcadian, was closely related to that of a very remote area, Cyprus. But Cyprus was known from archaeological evidence to have been colonized by Mycenaeans in the fourteenth and thirteenth centuries B.C. Thus it was almost certain that Arcadian and Cypriot together represented the relics of a Mycenaean dialect, spoken all over the pre-Dorian Peloponnese. This deduction supplied a very important control on the attempts to decipher a Mycenaean script as Greek. Any solution seriously out of line with Arcadian would have little chance of being right.

We must now describe in some detail the writing which Evans found in Crete, and related discoveries elsewhere. Evans was soon able to distinguish three phases in the history of Minoan writing,

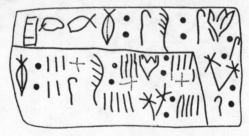

Fig. 3. Hieroglyphic tablet from Phaistos.

as he called it. In the earliest phase, dated very roughly to 2000–1650 B.C., the script consisted of pictorial signs, representing generally recognizable objects, such as a head, a hand, a star, an arrow and so forth. This was the script of the seal-stones, but Evans also found a few examples on lumps of clay used as sealings and clay bars. He named this style 'hieroglyphic', since the signs were of the same type as the early pictorial script of Egypt; there is little to show that the script was actually learnt from an Egyptian source. A hieroglyphic tablet from Phaistos is illustrated in Fig. 3. Comparison with similar Linear B tablets suggests that it records quantities of four commodities, probably wheat, oil, olives and figs. No attempt can be made at a real decipherment, because there is too little material, but the similarities make it clear that the system is closely allied to, and presumably the origin of, the next stage. This dates roughly from 1750 to 1450 B.C., perhaps beginning even earlier. Since the pictorial signs are now reduced to mere outlines, Evans named it Linear A. The direction of writing is from left to right. Examples of this have been found all over Crete, but not outside it, if we except the potters' marks found on pots at Melos and Thera. There are a number of inscriptions on stone and bronze objects—a feature strangely lacking in Linear B. The largest single collection of documents, however, is a group of about 150 clay tablets from a palace a few miles from Phaistos, known in the absence of an ancient name by that of the adjacent chapel of Hagia Triada (Holy Trinity). It is quite clear that these are mainly records of agricultural produce. One is illustrated in Fig. 4.

Fig. 4. Linear A tablet from Hagia Triada (no. 114).

At some date, which cannot yet be precisely determined, Linear A was replaced by a modified form of the script which Evans named Linear B. The date of this change would be highly significant; but unfortunately Linear B has so far been found at only one site in Crete, and although the documents using it are firmly dated to the destruction of the Late Minoan II palace, about 1400 B.C., it is not clear when Linear A went out of use there. It has been suggested that Linear A at Phaistos overlaps Linear B at Knossos; but comparative dating by archaeological means is impossible with the accuracy required. It is by no means incredible that there should be this overlap, but it remains a hypothesis which cannot yet be tested. As far as the available evidence goes, we can only say that Linear A seems to fade out about 1450 B.C., if indeed it survived as long as that.

The relationship between the two systems is perplexing. It is not simply a matter of reducing the early pictorial signs to simpler and more easily written forms, for in some instances the Linear B forms are more elaborate than their Linear A counterparts. Evans suggested that Linear B was a 'royal' orthography, developed by the Palace scribes and therefore employed exclusively at Knossos. This theory is now disproved by the discovery of Linear B in mainland Greece, and we can now see that Linear B is the result of adapting the Minoan script for the writing of Greek—though this could not be guessed at the time of its discovery. Even so this is only a partial explanation. There is no reason to change the form of a sign in order to write a new language, though it may be necessary to add or subtract, or change the values of some signs. French is written with basically the same alphabet as English, though there are certain additional letters ($à$, $ê$, etc.), k and w are virtually ignored, and some letters have different sounds. The differences between Linear A and Linear B are more like those between the Greek and Roman alphabets (e.g. $A = A$, $B = B$, but $\Gamma = G$, $\Delta = D$). Whether this parallel extends to the use of the same sign with different values (as Greek $X = kh$, Roman $X = x$) cannot be determined failing a decipherment of Linear A. It should be noted that all attempts at deciphering it so far published depend upon substituting Linear B values for Linear A signs, and therefore cannot answer this question. The differences make some of the identifications conjectural, and suggest that Linear B had a history of development between the original adaptation and the earliest texts. The fact that the earliest known texts are actually the Cretan ones may well be a false scent.

Though superficially alike, differences between the scripts are clear to a practised eye; a very obvious difference is that the guide lines or rules that separate the lines of writing on Linear B tablets are usually absent in Linear A. A further difference concerns the numerical system: in general this is very similar, but the treatment of fractional quantities is quite different. Linear A has a system of fractional signs, not yet fully worked out; Linear B has no signs of this type, but records fractional quantities in terms of smaller units, like pounds, shillings and pence, or dollars and cents, or tons, hundredweights, quarters and pounds. The divergence of the systems of measurement was demonstrated with admirable clarity by Professor E. L. Bennett Jr. in 1950.

In calling attention to these differences between A and B, Bennett was in effect attacking a view propounded by Evans and supported by the Italian scholar Professor G. Pugliese Carratelli, who published the most important series of Linear A texts in 1945. This was a theory that the language of the two systems was identical, and that the new script represented a later modification, like the modern roman type which is now replacing the clumsy 'Gothic' type formerly used for printing German. The evidence of identity of language, however, was exceedingly meagre. Not one word of any length was identical in the two scripts, though a small number of two- or three-sign words appeared to repeat, and others had similar beginnings and endings. The striking evidence against identity came from the recognition of the totalling formula, which will be discussed later (p. 46); there was plainly no resemblance between A and B in this.

Almost all the clay tablets found at Knossos were in Linear B, and the total number of tablets now known, including of course many small fragments, is between three and four thousand. All these tablets apparently came from the palace built in the period called by the archaeologists Late Minoan II, which was destroyed by fire at the end of the fifteenth century B.C. Minoan architecture made use of large quantities of timber, and even masonry walls were tied together by a system of timber baulks, rather like medieval timbering in structure; it is thought that the use of wood in this way gives a building flexibility to withstand earthquakes. The disadvantage, however, is that if it catches fire it burns fiercely; but this heat served to bake many of the clay tablets to the hardness of pottery, and so made them durable. There is no doubt that, contrary to the practice in Anatolia and farther East, the tablets in the Aegean area were never deliberately fired. The clay was moulded to the required shape, inscribed and left to dry; in summer, at least, a few hours would suffice to render them hard enough to store and no further writing could then be added. When no longer required the tablet could be 'pulped' by pounding it to fragments in water, and the clay used again.

The physical appearance of the tablets is unattractive. They are flat lumps of clay, usually dull grey in colour, though in some cases sufficient oxygen penetrated to the tablet while it was being burnt to cause oxidation, giving a pleasant red brick colour. They vary in size from small sealings and labels little more than an inch across to heavy page-shaped tablets as much as 10 inches by 5 inches. Many were found in a crumbly condition, and Evans had an unfortunate experience once when he left a freshly excavated batch in a storeroom overnight, the rain came through the roof, and there was nothing left in the morning but muddy lumps of clay. Such things were not, we may hope, allowed to happen again; but tablets are not easy to recover from the earth, and it is not impossible that some of the early excavators may have thrown them away as useless clods.

The abundance of tablets found at Knossos gave Evans high hopes of solving the riddle. In his earliest report, written in 1901, he noted the obvious facts about the script:

From the frequency of ciphers on these tablets it is evident that a great number of them refer to accounts relating to the royal stores and arsenal. The general purport of the tablet, moreover, is in many cases supplied by the introduction of one or more pictorial figures. Thus on a series of tablets, from the room called after them the Room of the Chariot Tablets, occur designs of a typical Mycenaean chariot, a horse's head and what seems to be a cuirass....Among other subjects thus represented were human figures, perhaps slaves, houses or barns, swine, ears of corn, various kinds of trees, saffron flowers, and vessels of clay of various shapes.... Besides these were other vases of metallic forms—implements such as spades, single-edged axes, and many indeterminate objects....

In the present incomplete state of the material it is undesirable to go beyond a very general statement of the comparison attainable. Among the linear characters or letters in common use—about 70 in number—10 are practically identical with signs belonging to the Cypriote syllabary[1] and about the same number show affinities to later Greek letter-forms.... The words on the tablets are at times divided by upright lines, and from the average number of letters included between these it is probable that the signs have a syllabic value. The inscriptions are invariably written from left to right.[2]

Evans does not, however, either at this time or subsequently, seem to have had any clear plan for the solution of the script. His suggestions were in many cases sound, but they were disjointed observations and he never laid down any methodical procedure. With great enthusiasm he set about arranging for the publication of his inscriptions, and persuaded the Clarendon Press to cast a special fount of 'Mycenaean' characters—the name 'Minoan' was only adopted later. Although subsequent additions were made to this fount it never became a wholly satisfactory means of printing Linear B; many of the characters in it are simple variants of one character without any significance, and the discovery of new texts outside Crete increased the repertoire. The few books now printed with Linear B texts mostly use a normalized hand-written transcript which is photographically reproduced.

The first volume of Minoan inscriptions, entitled *Scripta Minoa I*, was published in 1909. This was devoted to the hieroglyphic script, though it contained some allusions to the Linear scripts which were to form the subject of a second and a third volume. A good deal of the preparatory work was done for these in the following years; but Evans' enthusiasm for publication seems to have waned; the First World War supervened and the project was if not actually abandoned at least relegated in favour of a greater

---

[1] See below, p. 22.   [2] *Annual of British School at Athens*, IV, pp. 57-9.

and more urgent task, that of putting on record the whole story of
the successive Palaces of Knossos, and with them the first attempt
to define and describe the Minoan civilization. Of this story the
scripts formed only a minor part—and an unsatisfactory part,
since no real progress had been made in their decipherment.
Regrettable as this delay was, it must be admitted in the light of
our present knowledge that the chances of a successful decipherment were very small, even had all the material been made immediately available. But it is certain that some progress could
have been made, and much of the unprofitable speculation of the
next fifty years saved by a rapid publication.

A few tablets had been published in the initial dig reports and
other articles. A total of 120 became available when the vast work
on the *Palace of Minos* reached its fourth volume in 1935. About
the same time the Finnish scholar Professor Johannes Sundwall
visited Crete and succeeded in copying thirty-eight more; these
he published, together with some interesting speculations on their
significance. But this act of piracy cost him Evans' severe dis-
pleasure. It is an unwritten law among archaeologists that the
discoverer of any object has the right to be the first to publish it;
equitable as it seems, it can become absurd if an excavator refuses
to delegate the task of publication and delays it himself unduly.
Such cases are rare, but not entirely unknown, even in the more
co-operative international spirit which happily prevails among
archaeologists today.

Evans eventually died, at the age of ninety, in 1941, just in time
to be spared the news of the German occupation of Crete. His own
house, the Villa Ariadne at Knossos, became the headquarters of
the German command on the island. But *Scripta Minoa II* still
lay incomplete and in confusion among Evans' notes; and the task
of publication was then taken up anew by his old friend and
companion Sir John Myres, now retired from his chair at Oxford.
Much of the rest of Myres' life was devoted to this unrewarding
and arduous work. In the difficult post-war years the Clarendon

Press could not be expected to relish the prospect of printing an extremely difficult book in a script and language no one could read. The design of publishing the Linear A inscriptions was dropped, since this had already been admirably done by Professor Pugliese Carratelli. But the Linear B tablets were in Iraklion, and Myres was now too old and infirm to visit Greece again. In any case it was not until 1950 that conditions there became normal enough to permit the re-opening of museums; in Iraklion itself the new Museum had to be built, and some of the contents had suffered damage during the war.

Myres did succeed in getting a few scholars to do some checking for him; the Americans Dr Alice Kober and Dr Emmett L. Bennett generously put their work at his disposal. But no systematic check was possible until it was too late. It was not until some time after the publication of *Scripta Minoa II* in 1952 that it became clear how vital this check was. Myres is to be thanked for having pushed through the publication in the face of great difficulties; he was, however, reduced to reliance on Evans' transcripts and drawings, the accuracy of which left much to be desired. Evans again is not wholly to blame; it is exceedingly difficult to copy accurately an inscription in unfamiliar characters, and in any case the work seems usually to have been done by one of his draughtsman assistants.

But by this time the problem had been transformed by new discoveries. A full account of these must wait until the next chapter; in the meantime we must complete this account of the various Minoan scripts.

No account of writing in Crete would be complete without a mention of the famous Phaistos Disk. This was found by the Italian excavators of the Minoan Palace at Phaistos in southern Crete in 1908. It is a flat disk of baked clay, about 6½ inches in diameter, inscribed on both sides with a text which runs spirally from the rim to the centre, filling all the available space. The signs are pictorial and number forty-five; the direction of writing is from right to left. But the most remarkable feature of the disk is its method of execution. Each sign was separately impressed on the soft clay by means of a punch or type cut for the purpose. It is clear that the whole operation was not completed at once; only one of each of the set of punches was needed; nevertheless, this use of standard forms was a remarkable anticipation of the invention of engraving and printing. It is hard to believe that the preparation of this set of forty-five punches was undertaken solely for the production of one disk—so useful an invention would surely have been exploited. Moreover, the skill with which all the available space is filled argues some practice in the maker. But the disk remains so far unique. Attempts have been made to identify the signs with those of the hieroglyphic script, and some likenesses can be detected; it is more often, however, considered an import, from Anatolia according to Evans. But nothing like it in form or technique has yet been found anywhere in the ancient world. The possibility of decipherment therefore remains beyond our grasp, though this has not deterred a long succession of scholars and amateurs from producing their own versions, some of which will be quoted in the next chapter.

There is yet another ramification of the Minoan script proper. Between the two wars the accumulation of finds made it clear that during the Bronze Age a related script was in use in Cyprus, and it was therefore named Cypro-Minoan. The chief site of this period so far explored is a large and important city on the east coast of the island called by the modern name Enkomi. Excavation of this site is still continuing (1957), and it is almost certain that the writing found to date is but a small sample of what is still to come. Material of very different dates has come to light; the oldest is a small scrap of a tablet dated to the early fifteenth century B.C., a date which, if exact, makes Cypro-Minoan older than Linear B. The signs are different from any other form of the Minoan script, but suggest affinities with Linear A. Then come a group of tablets, mostly badly preserved, dated about the twelfth century B.C. These show a script in which the simplest signs are almost identical with the two Cretan scripts, but all the more complicated signs have been greatly modified, the elegant fine lines and curves of Linear A and B being abandoned in favour of heavy bars and dots. Now it requires some skill and a needle-sharp stylus to write Linear B on a clay surface; no people who habitually wrote on clay and nothing else would be likely to maintain the script in this form for long; it must have kept this form in Crete and Greece because it was also written with a pen or brush on a material such as paper.

Fig. 5. The development of cuneiform script.

But if, as was common in the Near East, clay was adopted in Cyprus as the principal writing material, then a modification such as we in fact see here would have been almost inevitable. A thicker, blunter stylus can be used, writing becomes much faster, and the size of the characters can be reduced—an important economy with such a bulky material as clay. A precisely similar development can be seen in the history of the cuneiform script in Babylonia; the early characters, which are recognizable pictograms, later become reduced to formalized patterns consisting of only three wedge-shaped strokes (see Fig. 5). It is consistent with this theory of a change in the normal writing material that the clay tablets of Cyprus were baked, not merely sun-dried as those of Greece. In form, too, they resemble much more closely the Oriental type. Similar to this Cypro-Minoan, but easily distinguished from it, is a form of the script found recently at the ancient city of Ugarit, the modern Ras Shamra, on the coast of Syria. This city used Akkadian cuneiform for most of its foreign correspondence, and had a unique cuneiform 'alphabet' to write its own Semitic speech; but it is not surprising that there was a Cypriot colony living there who used the script of their homeland. It must be emphasized that most of the evidence for these scripts has only been found in the last few years, and played no part in the decipherment of Linear B. They are still undeciphered and likely to remain so until more texts are found.

This digression, however, is not entirely irrelevant, for there is another Cypriot script which played a large part in the decipherment of Linear B. This is the classical Cypriot script, which was used to write Greek from at least the sixth century down to the third or second century B.C. It was solved in the 1870's, the first steps being due to an Englishman, George Smith; the key to it lay in the bilingual inscriptions in this and Phoenician, and in the script and the Greek alphabet. There are a number of inscriptions written in it which are clearly not Greek, but an unknown language. The system revealed is illustrated in Fig. 6. Each sign represents, not a single letter, but a whole syllable: either a plain vowel (*a e i o u*), or a consonant plus vowel. The consonants in use are *j* (= English *y*), *k*, *l*, *m*, *n*, *p*, *r*, *s*, *t*, *w*, *x* and *z*, but not all combinations of these consonants and vowels are actually found. Such a system is most inconvenient for Greek. The stops *k*, *p* and *t* have each to do duty for three sounds represented by separate letters of the Greek alphabet: thus *k* represents *k*, *g* and *kh*, *p* = *p*, *b* and *ph*, *t* = *t*, *d* and *th*. (It may come as a surprise to those who know a little Greek that *kh*, *ph* and *th* were in ancient Greek pronounced not as in lo*ch*, *ph*ial, and *th*ink, but as in blo*ckh*ead, Cla*ph*am and a*t h*ome; that is why the Romans transcribed the Greek *ph* at first as *p*, and later as *ph*, but never as *f*.) Secondly, there is no means of showing groups of consonants or final consonants. This had to be done by adding 'dead' or unpronounced vowels, their quality being taken from the following or preceding vowel, though at the end of a word *e* is always used; *n* before another consonant is simply omitted. As a result the Greek word *anthrōpos*, 'man', is written *a-to-ro-po-se*; there is no way of showing the long vowels ē and ō, which have special signs in the Greek alphabet (η, ω).

Now classical Cypriot was obviously related to Linear B. Seven signs can be easily equated, and there are others showing varying degrees of resemblance, but about three-quarters of the signs

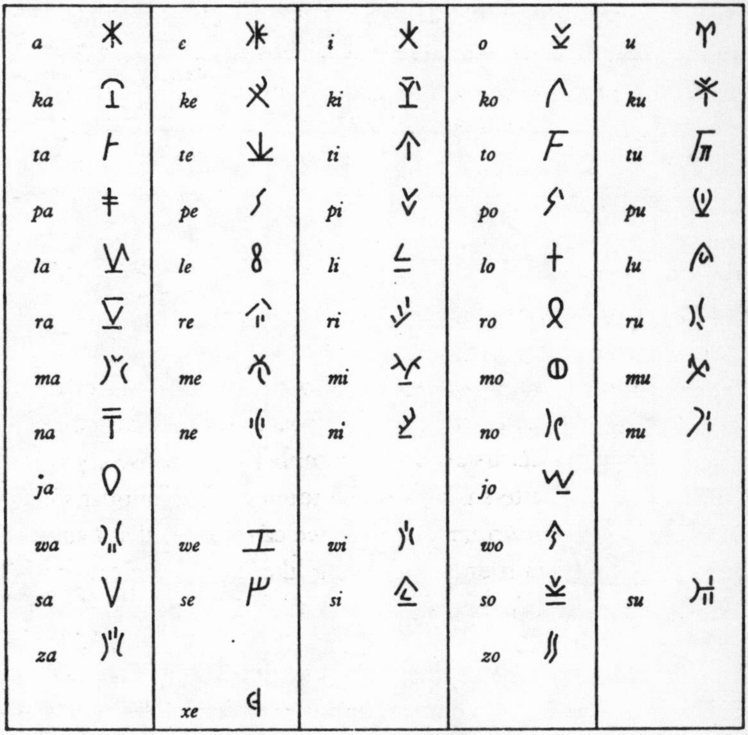

Fig. 6. The Cypriot syllabary.

could only be equated by pure guesswork, and we now know that most of the guesses were wrong. For instance, in the table drawn up by Myres in *Scripta Minoa II*, out of thirty-two Linear B signs only eleven are right or nearly right. None the less, almost all who approached Linear B started by transferring the Cypriot values to the Linear B signs, though even the most elementary study of the history of writing shows that the same sign, even in related systems, may stand for different sounds.

The Cypriot clue was confusing in another way too. It was too readily assumed that the spelling conventions of Linear B would be similar to those of Cypriot; this led to an important deduction. The most common final consonant in Greek is *s*. Thus a high proportion of words in Cypriot end in -*se*, *e* being the 'dead'

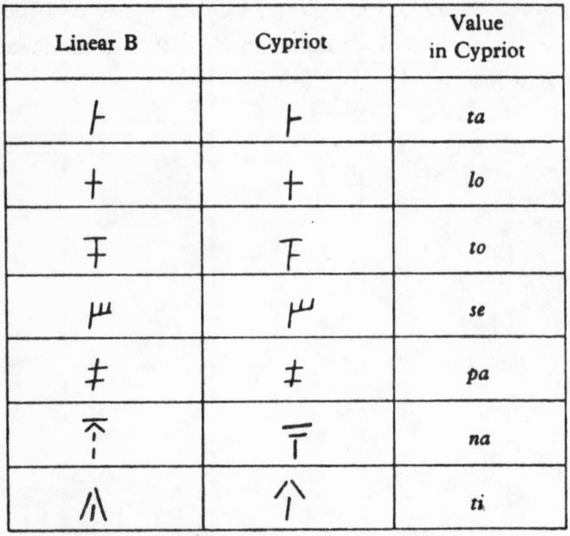

Linear B	Cypriot	Value in Cypriot
� symbol	⊢	*ta*
+	+	*lo*
⊤	Ⴀ	*to*
⊬	⊬	*se*
⧧	⧧	*pa*
⊼	⊤	*na*
⋀	⋀	*ti*

Fig. 7. Comparison of signs in Linear B and Classical Cypriot.

vowel. Now *se* is one of the few signs immediately recognizable in Linear B (see Fig. 7); but this sign is very rare as the ending of a word in Linear B, nor does any sign show this characteristic distribution. It could thus be argued that the language of Linear B could hardly be Greek.

Here was the internal evidence to support the conclusion drawn by Evans from the archaeological record, that the culture of Minoan Crete was totally different from that of Mycenaean Greece, whether or not the latter was Greek in the sense of speaking the Greek language. The influence of Evans and his followers was immense. Only a very few archaeologists dared to question the orthodox doctrine, and the most courageous, the late A. J. B. Wace, who was to become Professor of Classical Archaeology in the University of Cambridge, paid dearly for his heretical views; he was excluded from digging in Greece for a considerable period. The voices raised in dissent were crying in the wilderness, and although mainland influence was beginning to be admitted in Late Minoan Crete, Ventris' proof that the masters of Knossos spoke Greek came as an electrifying shock to almost all who had studied the question.

CHAPTER 3

HOPES AND FAILURES

The success of any decipherment depends upon the existence and availability of adequate material. How much is needed depends upon the nature of the problem to be solved, the character of the material, and so forth. Thus a short 'bilingual' inscription, giving the same text in two languages, may be used as a crib, and may supply enough clues to enable the rest of the material to be interpreted. Where, as in this case, no bilingual exists, a far larger amount of text is required. Moreover, restrictions may be imposed by the type of text available; for instance, the thousands of Etruscan funerary inscriptions known have permitted us to gain only a very limited knowledge of the language, since the same phrases are repeated over and over again.

There are two methods by which one can proceed. One is by a methodical analysis, and this approach will form the subject of the next chapter; the other is by more or less pure guesswork. Intelligent guessing must of course play some part in the first case; but there is a world of difference between a decipherment founded upon a careful internal analysis and one obtained by trial and error. Even this may produce the correct result; but it needs to be confirmed by application to virgin material, since it can gain no probability from its origin. A cool judgement is also needed to discriminate between what a text is likely or unlikely to contain. This faculty was notably lacking among those who risked their reputations on the conjectural method.

Evans and the more cautious of his followers had observed that with few apparent exceptions all the documents were lists or accounts. The reasons for this will be discussed later on. But this did not prevent some amateurs from venturing upon interpretations of their own. In most cases these would-be decipherers began by guessing the language of the inscriptions—most of them treated A and B and even the Phaistos Disk as all specimens of the same language. Some chose Greek, though the Greek which they obtained would not stand philological examination. Others chose a language with obscure affinities or one imperfectly known: Basque and Etruscan were proposed as candidates. Others again invented languages of their own for the purpose, a method which had the advantage that no one could prove them wrong. One attempt, by the Bulgarian Professor V. Georgiev, presented an ingenious *mélange* of linguistic elements, which resembled Greek when it suited his purpose and any other language when it did not. Almost all decipherers made resemblances with the Cypriot script their starting-point.

It would be tedious and unnecessary to discuss here all the attempts published up to 1950; a few samples of translations proposed should be enough to illustrate the nature of a good deal of the work on this problem.

The Czech scholar Professor Bedřich Hrozný established a deserved reputation for himself by his demonstration, about the time of the First World War, that the Hittite language written in a cuneiform script was in fact of Indo-European origin, thus opening the way to its study. His subsequent work unfortunately was not all as successful as this, and in his latter years he commenced an attack on all the unsolved scripts known to him. The Indus valley script—a prehistoric script of Northern India—was quickly 'solved'; he then turned to Minoan, and in 1949 produced a lengthy monograph.[1] He collected all the inscriptions published to date, including some from Pylos, and without any discussion of method proceeded to interpret them. His method, as far as it can be observed, was to compare the Minoan signs with the signs of other scripts—not merely classical Cypriot, but Egyptian, Hieroglyphic Hittite, Proto-Indian (the Indus valley script), Cuneiform, and Phoenician and other early alphabets. It is of course only too

---

[1] *Les Inscriptions Crétoises, Essai de déchiffrement* (Prague, 1949).

27

easy to find something in one of the scripts which looks vaguely like something in Linear B—and some of the resemblances are far-fetched indeed. The other essential for the success of this method was that the language should turn out to be a kind of Indo-European language akin to Hittite. Without some such assumption the mere substitution of phonetic values would have been useless.

Here is his version of a Pylos text (given in English translation of the French of his publication):

Place of administration Ḫataḫuâ: the palace has consumed all (?).

Place of administration Saḫur(i)ta (is) a bad (?) field (?): this (delivers in) tribute 22 (?) (measures), 6 T-measures of saffron capsules (p. 304).

We now translate this text as follows:

Thus the priestess and the key-bearers and the Followers and Westreus (hold) leases: so much wheat 21·6 units.

The arbitrariness of Hrozný's work is so patent that no one has taken it seriously. It is a sad story which recurs too often in the world of scholarship: an old and respected figure produces in his dotage work unworthy of his maturity, and his friends and pupils have not the courage to tell him so.

In 1931 a small volume was published by the Oxford University Press entitled *Through Basque to Minoan*. Its author was F. G. Gordon, and he endeavoured to read Minoan by 'assigning Basque values to the characters, on the chance that the two languages might be nearly related'. The choice of Basque was dictated by the reasoning that Minoan was probably not Indo-European, and Basque is the only non-Indo-European language surviving in Europe which was not introduced in historical times.

His method is a popular one among the dilettanti. Each sign is first identified as an object, however vague the resemblance; this object is then given its name in the language assumed, and the sign is solved. Gordon was content to stay at this stage, regarding each sign as meaning a word. Others advanced further by using the 'acrophonic' principle: this means that the sign may represent only the first part, or the first letter, of the word.

Gordon translated on this basis a few Knossos inventories as elegiac poems, reading the signs from left to right or right to left as suited his convenience, and even turning one tablet upside down, so that a pictogram of a chariot-frame could be misinterpreted as 'an ovoid vase lying on its side, supported on two feet, and pouring out liquid' (p. 42). But when he turned to the Phaistos Disk he excelled himself. Here are a few lines from his translation:

...the lord walking on wings the breathless path, the star-smiter, the foaming gulf of waters, dogfish smiter on the creeping flower; the lord, smiter of the horse-hide (*or* the surface of the rock), the dog climbing the path, the dog emptying with the foot the water-pitchers, climbing the circling path, parching the wine-skin...(pp. 55–6).

The same year saw another similar venture, by Miss F. Melian Stawell, in a book called modestly *A Clue to the Cretan Scripts* (Bell, London, 1931). Using the acrophonic principle mentioned above, she dealt with a great deal of the hieroglyphic script, the Phaistos Disk and some Linear A inscriptions. Little effort was made to interpret the Linear B tablets, except for a few formulas; she recognized that these were inventories and wisely kept to inscriptions whose sense was not obvious.

She started with the assumption that Evans was wrong and the Minoan language was in fact Greek. She named the objects in Greek, using some odd and even invented words, and extracted a syllabic value by abbreviating these. Each sign-group in the Phaistos Disk (obviously a word) is expanded to form a phrase, thus: *an-sa-kŏ-tĕ-re*. This is then expanded into what Miss Stawell thought was Greek:

> *Ana, Saō; koō, thea, Rē*
> Arise, Saviour! Listen, Goddess, Rhea!

She admitted the Greek was hardly archaic enough; clearly she knew little of what archaic Greek would look like. All her interpretations are similarly arbitrary.

Another attempt was made on the Phaistos Disk by the Greek scholar K. D. Ktistopoulos. It is only fair to say at once that he has also done some very useful statistical work on sign frequency in the Linear scripts. But here is part of his translation of the Disk, which he interprets as a Semitic language:

> Supreme—deity, of the powerful thrones star,
> supreme—tenderness of the consolatory words,
> supreme—donator of the prophecies,
> supreme—of the eggs the white....[1]

It does not need the author's apology for inexpertness in Semitic philology to make us suspect that something has gone wrong here.

One of the superficially most promising attempts at reading a Minoan text as Greek was made in 1930 by the Swedish archaeologist Professor Axel Persson. Four years earlier an expedition under his direction had found in a late Mycenaean tomb at Asine, near Nauplia in the north-east of the Peloponnese, a jar with what appears to be an inscription on the rim. He compared these signs with those of the classical Cypriot syllabary, and on this basis transcribed a few words. With one exception these looked little like Greek; but *po-se-i-ta-wo-no-se* was a plausible form, assuming the Cypriot spelling rules, for the Greek *Poseidāwōnos*, genitive of the name of the god Poseidon. Unfortunately, those expert in the Minoan scripts have been unable to share Persson's confidence in his identifications. The signs on the jar are quite unlike Linear B or any other known Bronze Age script, and it requires a good deal of imagination to see the resemblance to the classical Cypriot syllabary. In fact Ventris after a careful examination of the original came to the conclusion that the marks are not writing at all; they may be a kind of doodling, or possibly an attempt by an illiterate person to reproduce the appearance of writing. The lack of regularity and clear breaks between the signs is obvious, and at one end it tails off into a series of curves, which look more like a decorative pattern. It is interesting to observe that the form of the

[1] Paper submitted to the Academy of Athens, 27 May 1948.

name read by Persson is now known to be wrong for the Mycenaean dialect, in which it appears as *po-se-da-o-no*.

Of a very different character was the work of the Bulgarian V. Georgiev, who summed up a series of earlier publications in a book entitled (in Russian) *Problems of the Minoan Language* published in Sofia in 1953. He dealt somewhat scornfully with his critics, but recognized that his theory would take a long time to perfect and could not convince everyone at once. The Minoan language was, he believed, a dialect of a widespread pre-Hellenic language spoken in Greece before the coming of the Greeks and possibly related to Hittite and other early Anatolian languages. This theory, which in one form or another has enjoyed considerable popularity, undoubtedly contains an element of truth, though we are still unable to say how much. One thing that is certain is that most Greek place-names are not composed of Greek words: there are a few that are, like *Thermopulai* 'Hot-gates', but a good number, like *Athēnai* (Athens), *Mukēnai* (Mycenae), *Korinthos, Zakunthos, Halikarnassos, Lukabēttos*, are not only devoid of meaning, but belong to groups with a restricted range of endings; just as English names can be recognized by endings like *-bridge*, *-ton*, *-ford*. The preservation of place-names belonging to an older language is a common phenomenon: in England many Celtic names survive, such as the various rivers called *Avon* (Welsh *afon* 'river'), though Celtic has not been spoken in their neighbourhood for more than a thousand years. The attempt has therefore been made to establish the pre-Hellenic language of Greece through the medium of these place-names; but although the fact of its existence is clear, its nature is still very much disputed.

Georgiev believed that the language of the tablets was largely archaic Greek, but containing a large number of pre-Hellenic elements. This gave him liberty to interpret as Greek, or quasi-Greek, any word which suited him, while anything that did not make sense as Greek could be explained away. It must be said that the Greek was often of a kind unrecognizable by trained philologists without the aid of Georgiev's commentary. For instance a phrase from a Knossos tablet (Fp7) is transcribed: θetáaranà *make* and translated 'to the great grandmother-eagle', though the resemblance to Greek words is far to seek. For comparison the present version of the same phrase is: *ka-ra-e-ri-jo me-no* 'in the month of Karaerios'. Not a single sign has the same value. It is only fair to add that, after an initial period of hesitation, Georgiev has now fully accepted Ventris' theory.

In about 1950 a new method was tried by the German scholar Professor Ernst Sittig. He took the Cypriot inscriptions which are not in Greek and analysed the frequency of the signs; then, assuming the affinity of this Cypriot language with Minoan, he identified the Linear B signs on a combination of their statistical frequency and their resemblance to the Cypriot syllabary. The idea was good, but unfortunately the basic assumption that the languages were related was wrong; and it would have needed more material than he had available to establish accurate frequency patterns. Of fourteen signs that he considered certainly identified by this means, we now know that only three were right. This method can in suitable circumstances offer valuable help; but there must be no doubt about the identity of the language and the spelling conventions.

There were, however, some exceptions to this catalogue of failures; notably those who confined themselves to such observations as could be made without claiming a solution of the whole problem. Evans himself set a high standard. Believing as he did that the Minoan language was not Greek and unlikely to resemble any hitherto known, he was not tempted by rash theories. He was sufficiently acquainted with other ancient scripts not to fall into some traps, though in one respect this led him astray.

A prominent feature of certain cuneiform and other scripts is the use of what are called 'determinatives'. These are signs which do not represent a sound but serve to classify the word to which they are added; thus the name of every town begins with the determinative sign meaning TOWN, of every man with that for MAN; similarly, all objects of wood have a special sign, and so forth. In a complicated script this is a very important clue to the meaning of a word; by classifying it the possible readings are narrowed down and it is much easier to identify. A very simple form of determinative survives in English in our use of capital letters to mark out a proper name.

Evans thought he had detected this system of determinatives in Linear B. He observed that a large number of words began with 𐘚, a sign resembling a high-backed chair with a crook, which his vivid imagination interpreted as a throne and sceptre. Even more words began with 𐘅, which in a stylized form was plainly descended from the double-axe sign of the hieroglyphic script. This is a frequent motif in cult scenes, and had some religious significance. The next step was to guess that these two signs, in addition to their phonetic value, were when used as initials determinatives denoting 'royal' and 'religious' words: the one words connected with the palace administration; the other with the religious practices which were of great importance to the Minoans. Although this theory had few adherents among the experts— Hrozný was one—the prestige of Evans' name gave it some authority; it was in fact totally misleading. It depended upon mere guesswork, and a full analysis of the use of the signs would have shown a much more likely theory. The true explanation will appear in the next chapter.

A luckier shot emerged from Evans' attempt at using the Cypriot clue. A remarkable tablet, illustrated on Plate II, showed on two lines horse-like heads followed by numerals. The left-hand piece was not recorded by Evans; I identified it myself in Iraklion Museum in 1955 and joined it to the rest.[1] One head in each line was rather smaller and had no mane, and was preceded by the same two-sign word. These were both simple signs which could fairly safely be equated with similar Cypriot signs, reading

[1] See below, pp. 85–6.

po-lo. Now the Greek word for a 'foal' is *pōlos*; it is in fact related to the English *foal*, since by a change known to philologists as Grimm's law, *p-* in Greek is regularly represented by *f-* in certain Germanic languages including English. The coincidence was striking; but so convinced was Evans that Linear B could *not* contain Greek that he rejected this interpretation, though with obvious reluctance. It is now fashionable to give him credit for having interpreted this word; what a pity he was unwilling to follow up the clue on which he had stumbled.

Another sound piece of work was done in an article by A. E. Cowley published in 1927. Following a suggestion of Evans he discussed a series of tablets which dealt with women, since they were denoted by a self-evident pictogram. Following the entry for WOMEN there were other figures preceded by two words 𐘔𐘱 and 𐘔𐘲; it was not difficult to guess that these meant 'children', that is to say, 'boys' and 'girls', though there was at this time no means of determining which was which—Evans and Cowley were both wrong.

In 1940 a new name appears for the first time in the literature of the subject: Michael Ventris, then only eighteen years old. His article called 'Introducing the Minoan Language' was published in the *American Journal of Archaeology*; in writing to the editor he had been careful to conceal his age, but although in later years he dismissed the article as 'puerile', it was none the less soundly written. The basic idea was to find a language which might be related to Minoan. Ventris' candidate was Etruscan; not a bad guess, because the Etruscans, according to an ancient tradition, came from the Aegean to Italy. Ventris attempted to see how the Etruscan language would fit with Linear B. The results, as he admitted, were negative; but the Etruscan idea remained a fixation, which possessed him until in 1952 the Greek solution finally imposed itself on him. So firmly was Evans' Minoan theory based that at this date Greek seemed out of the question. 'The theory that Minoan could be Greek', Ventris wrote, 'is based

of course upon a deliberate disregard for historical plausibility.'
Hardly anyone would have ventured to disagree.

The most valuable contribution came a little later (1943–50),
from the American Dr Alice E. Kober. She died at the early age
of forty-three in 1950, just too soon to witness and take part in the
decipherment for which she had done so much to prepare the way.
She was the first to set out methodically to discover the nature of
the language through the barrier of the script. The questions she
asked were simple ones. Was it an inflected language, using different endings to express grammatical forms? Was there a consistent means of denoting a plural? Did it distinguish genders?

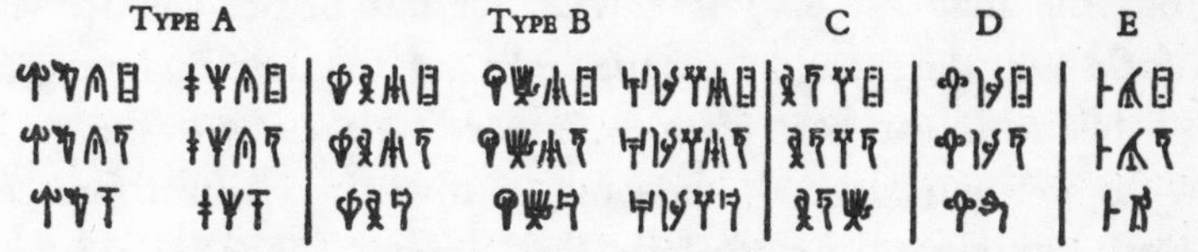

Fig. 8. 'Kober's triplets.'

Her solutions were partial, but none the less a real step forward.
She was able to demonstrate, for instance, that the totalling
formula, clearly shown by summations on a number of tablets,
had two forms: one was used for MEN and for one class of
animals, the other for WOMEN, another class of animals, and also
for swords and the like. This was not only clear evidence of a
distinction of gender; it also led to the identification of the means
by which the sex of animals is represented (that is, by adding
marks to the appropriate ideograms). Even more remarkable was
her demonstration that certain words had two variant forms,
which were longer than the·simple form by one sign. These are
now commonly, and irreverently, known as 'Kober's triplets'.
She interpreted them as further evidence of inflexion; but they
were destined to play an even more important role in the final
decipherment. I do not think there can be any doubt that Miss
Kober would have taken a leading part in events of later years,
had she been spared; she alone of the earlier investigators was

pursuing the track which led Ventris ultimately to the solution of the problem.

At this point we must take up again the history of discovery. Up to 1939 Linear B tablets were known only from one site, Knossos in Crete. But a small number of vases had been found in mainland Greece having inscriptions which had been painted on them before they were fired. These showed some variant forms, but had the same general appearance as Linear B. The presence of a Cretan script was not surprising, since on Evans' theory of a Minoan Empire Cretan imports might obviously be found at any site under Minoan control. The location of these sites can be seen from the map on p. 9 (Fig. 1). But just before the Second World War the situation was suddenly and dramatically reversed.

Schliemann had been led to Mycenae by believing in the truth of the Homeric legend; the obscure town of classical Greece, which sent eighty men to fight the Persians at Thermopylae in 480 B.C., had once been the capital of a great state. Could not other Homeric cities be located? This was the question in the mind of Professor Carl Blegen of the University of Cincinnati, who was already recognized as one of the foremost experts on the prehistoric period in Greece, and whose careful work on the site of Troy was justly famous. He set out now to find the palace of another Homeric monarch, Nestor, the garrulous old warrior whose name was a by-word for longevity.

Nestor ruled at Pylos; but where was Pylos? Even in classical times there was a proverb which ran: 'There is a Pylos before a Pylos and there is another besides.' The debate over Nestor's Pylos began with the Alexandrian commentators on Homer in the third century B.C. and has continued intermittently ever since. The geographer Strabo (first century A.D.) gives a long discussion of the problem; there were three likely candidates: one in Elis (north-west of the Peloponnese), one in Triphylia (centre of west coast), and one in Messenia (south-west). For various reasons Strabo picked on the Triphylian one, and a famous German archaeologist called Dörpfeld tried to clinch the matter in the early years of this century when he located some Mycenaean tombs at a place called Kakóvatos. But although tombs usually imply a residential site in the neighbourhood, no palace could be found.

Blegen resolved to pay no attention to Strabo and to explore the Messenian area. It was here that the modern town of Pylos is situated, at the south of the bay of Navarino—the scene of the famous naval engagement of 1827, when the British, French and Russian forces destroyed the Turkish and Egyptian fleets and thus struck a decisive blow for Greek independence. The ancient town of classical times was at the northern end of the bay, the site of a famous operation by the Athenians in the Peloponnesian War (425 B.C.). But Strabo records that this was not the original site, as the inhabitants had moved there from an earlier town 'under Mount Aigaleon'; unfortunately we do not know precisely which this mountain was, nor how close 'under' implies. Blegen found a likely site some four miles north of the bay at a place now called Epáno Englianós, and together with the Greek Dr Kourouniotis organized a joint American-Greek expedition to dig it in 1939. Blegen began work tentatively with the aid of one student, and by an astonishing piece of luck their first trial trench ran through what is now known as the archive room. Tablets were found within twenty-four hours, and the first season's work produced no fewer than 600 clay tablets, similar to the Knossos ones and written in the identical Linear B script. Here again war intervened and the excavation could not be resumed until 1952, when further finds of tablets were made. Subsequent digs have continued to increase slightly the number of texts known. The war prevented study and publication of the first finds; but it was possible to photograph the tablets before they were stored away in the vaults of the Bank of Athens, where they remained intact throughout the occupation. After the war Blegen entrusted their editing to Professor Emmett L. Bennett Jr., who has now become the world expert on the reading of Mycenaean texts. His edition, prepared from the photographs, appeared in 1951; a new edition, corrected from the original texts and containing also the more recent discoveries, appeared at the end of 1955. Further finds are still (1957) being made at this site.

To complete the history of the appearance of the texts we may anticipate a little and mention the discovery in 1952 by Professor Wace of the first tablets from Mycenae. These were found not in the royal palace, which had been dug by Schliemann and Tsoundas at the end of the last century, but in separate buildings or houses outside the walls of the acropolis or royal castle. A further find in 1954 brought the number of tablets from this site up to fifty.

Evans' reaction to the news of the tablets from Pylos is not recorded; he was then eighty-eight and he died before the matter could be discussed. But his followers, who included the vast majority of archaeologists in every country, were quick to think of explanations. 'Loot from Crete' was seriously proposed; but was it likely that a pirate or raider would carry away a bulky collection of fragile documents that he could not read? A more plausible theory was that the Mycenaean raiders had carried off from Crete the scribes who had kept the accounts of the Minoan palace and set them to work at their trade back at home. This would explain, at need, a Greek king keeping his accounts in Minoan, just as in the Middle Ages an English king might have his accounts kept in Latin. But it may be doubted whether anyone keeps accounts unless he needs to do so; an illiterate community will not import accountants unless the economic circumstances of its life change sufficiently to make them essential. A further idea was also mooted: that the Mycenaeans were not Greeks at all, but spoke some other language. The truth, that the Knossos tablets too were in Greek, was hardly considered.

Bennett, working on the new material, proceeded with sound sense and caution. He wrote a doctoral thesis on it, but this was not published. His article on the different system of weights and measures in Linear A and Linear B has been mentioned above.

But his outstanding contribution is the establishment of the signary; the recognition of variant forms and the distinction of separate signs. How difficult the task is only those who have tried can tell. It is easy enough for us to recognize the same letter in our alphabet as written by half a dozen different people, despite the use of variant forms. But if you do not know what is the possible range of letters, nor the sound of the words they spell, it is impossible to be sure if some of the rare ones are separate letters or mere variants. This is still the position with regard to Linear B. In the table printed at the end of the book nos. 18 and 19 occur only a few times; are they variants of no. 17 or not? It is to Bennett's credit that few such problems remain; diligent comparison enabled him to set up a table of variants which made it clear in the case of all but the rarest signs what was its possible range of variation. By contrast, it is one of the weaknesses of *Scripta Minoa II* that different signs are sometimes confused, and variants of the same are treated as distinct. At this time Ventris was already exchanging ideas with Bennett, and his suggestions must have contributed to the satisfactory outcome. Their correspondence laid the foundation of a friendship, which developed during Bennett's visits to Europe.

With the publication of *The Pylos Tablets* in 1951 the scene was set for the decipherment. Orderly analysis, begun by Miss Kober and Bennett, could now take the place of speculation and guesswork; but it required clear judgement to perceive the right methods, concentration to plod through the laborious analysis, perseverance to carry on despite meagre gains, and finally the spark of genius to grasp the right solution when at last it emerged from the painstaking manipulation of meaningless signs.

CHAPTER 4

BIRTH OF A THEORY

So far this account of Linear B has deliberately reproduced the chaotic state of our knowledge up to the end of the Second World War. It is now time to give a clear and detailed analysis of the script as it appeared to the investigators who began a fresh attack on it at this period. We must, however, begin with some preliminary observations on the nature of the problem and the methods which can be applied.

There is an obvious resemblance between an unreadable script and a secret code; similar methods can be employed to break both. But the differences must not be overlooked. The code is deliberately designed to baffle the investigator; the script is only puzzling by accident. The language underlying the coded text is ordinarily known; in the case of a script there are three separate possibilities. The language may be known or partially known, but written in an unknown script; this, for instance, was the case with the decipherment of the Old Persian inscriptions by the German scholar Grotefend in 1802; the cuneiform signs were then quite unknown, but the language, as revealed by recognition of proper names, turned out to be largely intelligible through the medium of the Avestan texts. Secondly, the script may be known, the language unknown. This is the case of Etruscan, which is written in a modified form of the Greek alphabet that presents little difficulty to the understanding of its sounds; but no language has yet been found sufficiently closely related to throw any light on the meaning of the words. Thus in spite of a large collection of inscriptions our knowledge of Etruscan is still very elementary and uncertain. Lastly, we have the situation which confronted the decipherers of the Minoan script, an unknown script *and* an unknown language. The fact that the language *subsequently* proved to be known is irrelevant; that fact could not be used in the first stages of the decipherment.

In the last case decipherments have usually been judged to be possible only when they could start from a bilingual text. The Egyptian hieroglyphs began to yield their secret only when the discovery of the Rosetta stone, with the Egyptian text repeated in Greek, made it possible to equate the royal names in the two versions. No such document exists for Minoan; but it was useless to sit back and wait for one to appear.

Cryptography has contributed a new weapon to the student of unknown scripts. It is now generally known that any code can in theory be broken, provided sufficient examples of coded texts are available; the only method by which to achieve complete security is to ensure continuous change in the coding system, or to make the code so complicated that the amount of material necessary to break it can never be obtained. The detailed procedures are irrelevant, but the basic principle is the analysis and indexing of coded texts, so that underlying patterns and regularities can be discovered. If a number of instances can be collected, it may appear that a certain group of signs in the coded text has a particular function; it may, for example, serve as a conjunction. A knowledge of the circumstances in which a message was sent may lead to other identifications, and from these tenuous gains further progress becomes possible, until the meaning of most of the coded words is known. The application of this method to unknown languages is obvious; such methods enable the decipherer to determine the *meaning* of sign-groups without knowing how to pronounce the signs. Indeed it is possible to imagine a case where texts in an unknown language might be understood without finding the phonetic value of a single sign.

The first step is of course to determine the type of system employed and, in the case of Linear B, this is not so difficult as it seems at first sight. There are only three basic ways of committing language to writing, and all known graphic systems use one or a combination of these. The simplest method is to draw a picture to represent a word; these pictograms are then often simplified until they become unrecognizable, but the principle remains that one sign represents one word. This is called 'ideographic' writing, and it has been carried to the highest stage of development by the Chinese, who still write in this way, although the Communist government is now trying to introduce reforms. For instance, 人 is 'man', 女 'woman'; non-pictorial concepts have of course to be expressed by oblique means: thus 大 is 'big'—it is a picture of the fisherman telling you how big the one was that got away!; or 目 'eye' (much modified) is equipped with a pair of legs 見 to mean 'see'. The significant fact about ideographic systems is that they require an enormous number of signs to cope with even a simple vocabulary. Every literate Chinese has to be able to read and write several thousand different signs, and the large dictionaries list as many as 50,000. Even in English we still use ideograms on a restricted scale. The numerals are the most conspicuous example: 5 is not a sign for the word 'five', but for the concept of five; and one can often see abbreviations like Charing ✠.

Ideograms of course give no direct clue to the pronunciation of the word, and in fact the different Chinese dialects pronounce the characters very differently. It is as if everyone in Europe wrote CANIS, but read this as *cane, chien, perro, dog, Hund, sobaka, skili* and so forth; just as 5 is read *cinque, cinq, cinco, five, fünf, piat', pende*, etc. The other two systems are both made up of elements which, taken together, represent the sound of the word. Thus a number of signs are needed to write all but the shortest words. The difference between them is that the units of sound represented by the signs may be either whole syllables (pronounceable) or single letters (partly unpronounceable abstractions). A syllabic system splits words up like a child's first reading book: thus *in-di-vi-du-al* would require five signs. The total number of signs needed is obviously much less than in the ideographic system; but it may still be high if a language, like English, uses many complicated groups of consonants. A word like *strength*, for instance, is from the syllabic point of view a single unit. A language like Japanese, however, which consists almost entirely of 'open' syllables, that is, ones ending in a vowel, can easily be written in the native *kana* syllabary, which contains forty-eight signs helped out by two diacritical marks. Thus ヒ ロ シ マ *Hi-ro-shi-ma* or ナ ガ サ キ *Na-ga-sa-ki*. Actual Japanese spelling is nothing like as simple as this implies, since it is a mixture of ideographic and syllabic scripts. But there is a parallel much nearer home, the classical Cypriot script discussed above (p. 22), which uses fifty-four signs.

Alphabetic writing is generally held to be a Semitic invention, though the Egyptian script pointed the way to it, and it was only fully developed by the Greeks. Its characteristic feature is the small number of signs needed. Thus we use twenty-six letters in English (some of them redundant, like *c*, *k*, and *q* all for the same sound in some words), and the more complicated alphabets rarely exceed the thirty-two of modern Russian.

Equipped with this knowledge we can turn to our Linear B texts. These consist of groups of signs separated by small vertical bars; the length of the groups varies from two to eight signs. Accompanying these in many cases are other signs which stand alone followed by a numeral; many of these are recognizable pictograms. It is easy to guess that single signs standing alone are probably ideographic, that is, representing a whole word; those used in groups are likely to be either syllabic or alphabetic. A count of these signs shows that they number about eighty-nine —the exact total is still disputed, because some are very rare, and it is not yet clear whether certain forms are separate signs or variants of others. But the number is significant; it is far too small for a wholly ideographic system, and it is much too large for an alphabet. It must therefore be syllabic, and a fairly simple form of syllabary like the Cypriot or Japanese, not the more complicated systems of the cuneiform script. This elementary deduction was neglected by many of the would-be decipherers.

The first step towards the solution was the explanation of the numerical and metrical systems. The numerals were straightforward, and were tabulated by Evans at an early stage. They are based on the decimal system, but are not positional; there is no notation for zero, and figures up to 9 are represented by repeating the sign the appropriate number of times, much as in Roman numerals. Vertical strokes denote digits, horizontal strokes tens, circles hundreds, circles with rays thousands, and circles with rays and a central bar tens of thousands. Thus 12,345 is written

$$⟡ 𝕏 ⊛° -- ⫴$$

The basis of the metrical system was worked out by Bennett in 1950. He showed that the signs ⚏, ⚌, ♯, ⚋, etc., constituted a system of weights, while other goods were recorded in the series ⊤, ◁, ▽ or ↑, ◁, ▽. As Bennett correctly guessed, the former series was used for dry measure, the latter for liquids. The use of the same symbols for the lower fractions is paralleled by the English use of *pint* and *quart* for both dry and liquid measure, the series thereafter diverging to *bushel* and *gallon*.

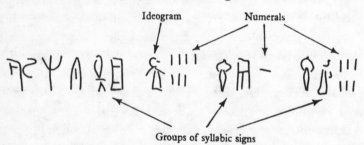

Fig. 9. Pylos tablet Aa62 showing composition of the text.

The signs on the tablets then could be divided into two classes: ideograms (together with metric signs and numerals) and syllabic signs. This will be clear by reference to Fig. 9. There is a complication, in that certain syllabic signs are also used as ideograms. But many of the ideographic signs are only used in this way with numerals, and by studying them Bennett was able to evolve a classification of the Pylos tablets, which groups together tablets dealing with similar subjects. Seen in the light of the decipherment this system was remarkably accurate, and the letter prefixes (*Aa*, *Cn*, *Sc*, etc.) devised by Bennett are still generally used in quoting the number of a text.

As will be apparent from Fig. 10 the meaning of some of these ideographic signs was obvious. But there was still a large number of signs too stylized to allow guesswork; though now that we have worked out the meaning by reference to the context, we can sometimes see their derivation. It was, however, possible to

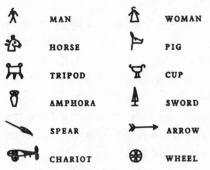

MAN

WOMAN

HORSE

PIG

TRIPOD

CUP

AMPHORA

SWORD

SPEAR

ARROW

CHARIOT

WHEEL

Fig. 10. Some obvious ideograms.

Fig. 11. Sex differentiation of the ideogram PIG.

classify many more of the ideograms with the help of those which could be recognized. Thus along with HORSE and PIG were regularly found three other ideograms which were therefore likely to belong to the same category of livestock. It was not easy to tell which was which, and here some understandable mistakes were made. It was also noticed that variants of the livestock ideograms occurred, the commonest being to modify the main vertical stroke or axis of the sign by adding two short cross bars, or dividing it into a fork (see Fig. 11). Evans correctly guessed that these signified male and female animals, but Sundwall reversed the sexes. Miss Kober finally settled the question by showing that the ideograms for men and male animals share one form of the word for 'total', while women and female animals

45

have another form; the distinction of men and women was of course clear.

Thus in many cases it was possible to deduce the general subject-matter of the tablets before a single syllable could be read; almost without exception it was clear that they were lists, inventories or catalogues. For instance, a list of single sign-groups ('words'), each followed by the ideogram MAN and the numeral 1, was clearly a list of men's names, a muster roll or the like. If the names were followed by WOMAN 1, then they sometimes had added small numbers of children, the word for which had been pointed out by Cowley (see p. 34). On the other hand, where a word was followed by MAN and a number larger than one, and this collocation was repeated on a number of different tablets, the word was likely to be a descriptive title or occupational term, like 'cow-herds', 'tailors' or 'men of Phaistos'. A similar series of words could be deduced for women. If a word is regularly associated with a particular ideogram, it is likely to be the name of the object denoted by that ideogram; but if there are several varying words associated with the same ideogram, then they may be epithets denoting the various types.

Other kinds of word are less easy to identify. But the words for 'total' have been mentioned several times already. These could be identified because a series of numbers was totalled at the bottom of the tablet, and thus the meaning of the word preceding this numerical total established.

This method of deduction, since it depends chiefly on studying the same words in different combinations, is often called 'combinatory'. Its usefulness is not exhausted at this stage, but it does even at the outset lead to some valuable conclusions about the meaning or sort of meaning possessed by certain words. At a later stage these can also act as a check on the correctness of a decipherment, because they are completely independent of the syllabic values. If a word so identified as an occupational term turns out, when transcribed phonetically, to mean 'cow-herds', this confirms the interpretation. On the other hand, interpretations which do not agree with this preliminary classification are at once suspect, due allowance being made for errors.

In order to work successfully on texts of this kind, it is essential to become completely familiar with their appearance. The signs must be thoroughly learnt, so that there is no risk of confusing one with another, and sign-groups and even portions of text must be committed to memory, so that similar groups elsewhere can be identified. Careful indexing will reveal the repetitions of identical sign-groups; but the most significant discoveries are often not the exact repetitions, but groups which are very much alike but show slight variations. Ventris laid great stress on the need for a good visual memory; in this, as in so much else, he was richly endowed.

Ventris' first contribution to the study of Linear B has been described in chapter 3. After the war, when he had completed his training as an architect, he returned to it with renewed vigour. At the beginning of 1950 he took the unusual step of circulating a questionnaire to a group of a dozen scholars of international reputation, whom he knew to be actively working on the Minoan scripts. The questions were drawn up to elicit opinions on the type of language or languages concealed by the scripts, any possible evidence of inflexion, the relationship of Linear A, Linear B and Cypriot, and so forth. It says a great deal, not only for international co-operation but also for the acuity of his questionnaire, that ten scholars supplied answers. These Ventris translated into English if necessary, and circulated at his own expense to all the rest, together with an analysis and his own views. The official title was: 'The Languages of the Minoan and Mycenaean Civilizations'; but since it was deliberately designed to review the position fifty years after Evans' discovery of the first tablets, it came to be known as the 'Mid-Century Report'.

The ten scholars who sent answers were Bennett (U.S.A.), Bossert and Grumach (Germany), Schachermeyr (Austria),

Pugliese Carratelli and Peruzzi (Italy), Georgiev (Bulgaria), Ktistopoulos (Greece), Sundwall (Finland), and Myres (Great Britain). There was the widest diversity in their views; Georgiev and Ktistopoulos both believed they had already achieved at least a partial solution. The others were reserved, but this exchange of opinions served to clear the air, and to show at least how little agreement there was on the basic issues.

The two who failed to reply were Hrozný (Czechoslovakia), who was by this time an old man, and had in any case recently published his own attempt at decipherment; and Miss Kober (U.S.A.), whose work was to prove so fruitful. She replied briefly that she thought the questionnaire was a waste of time; but this rebuff did not prevent Ventris from establishing friendly relations with her.

In one sense Miss Kober was right; the discussion of unproven theories is often barren, and much that was written at this time now seems unreal and blind. It is astonishing to think that no one then seriously contemplated Greek as a possible language for Linear B. Ventris suggested that even if there were some Greeks living on the mainland, the principal language was something else. The majority opinion was that it would prove to be a language of the Indo-European family, to which Greek belongs, but perhaps more closely related to Hittite. The minority view, to which Ventris himself adhered, was that it was an 'Aegean' language of a poorly known type, but probably represented by Etruscan.

The most interesting part of this document is the section by Ventris himself. In this he makes it plain that the first step must be to establish the relationships between alternating signs, independently of the phonetic values; all the rest, apart from Miss Kober, had concentrated attention on finding phonetic values, and the possibility of grouping the undeciphered signs had escaped them. The search for a pattern was the essential cryptographic procedure that made possible his success. The phonetic values proposed at this stage, by Ventris as well as others, were little more than guesses based on the Cypriot syllabary, and offered little prospect of progress. The truth was that sufficient material was lacking to permit sound conclusions.

Ventris intended his summing up to be the end of his own work on the problem for the time being. He had now a full-time job as an architect on the staff of the Ministry of Education, and he did not expect to be able to spare time and energy for the Minoan scripts. He ended the Report with these words: 'I have good hopes that a sufficient number of people working on these lines will before long enable a satisfactory solution to be found. To them I offer my best wishes, being forced by pressure of other work to make this my last small contribution to the problem.'

But it is not so easy to let a fascinating problem rest unsolved; it continues to fret one's mind at odd moments, and sooner or later one comes back to it, even at the expense of more urgent tasks. During the following two years Ventris, so far from letting it rest, followed up the Report with an intensive period of work on his own. It was typical of him that the series of twenty long Work Notes—in all 176 foolscap pages—that he prepared during this period were all duplicated and circulated (to a limited number of scholars) at his own expense. By means of these we are able to follow the complete history of the decipherment and the stages by which he reached it. No one could accuse him of having made up an account of his work afterwards so as to present a fortuitous discovery as the product of rational method. All the rough working, all the mistakes are exposed to view. It will of course be impossible to go through these notes in detail; here I shall pick out, especially from the later ones, what now seems interesting and significant, guided by the account he himself later wrote in *Documents in Mycenaean Greek*.

We are now approaching the critical stage, and it will be necessary to look at the problem much more closely. In the later Work Notes Ventris used in his discussion the actual signs of the

Linear B script, in a normalized form and beautifully drawn in his own hand—he was a first-rate draughtsman, and his handwriting had the regularity and clarity of printing, without, however, being devoid of character. In this book I have reluctantly decided not to follow this practice, not just because I am not so good at drawing, but for two good reasons: the difficulty of printing Minoan characters—no satisfactory fount of type yet exists for them, and each word would have to be made into a block and separately inserted in the text; and also the difficulty that most readers would find in identifying signs in a wholly unfamiliar script. Everyone knows that in a foreign script many of the letters tend to look alike, and some method has to be found to make the script readable and printable. I am therefore going to substitute for the signs the numbers which are now conventionally applied to them; this system is based upon Bennett's classification of the signs which groups together those built alike; a table of them will be found on the chart at the front of the book. Thus words will be quoted as successions of two-figure numbers, those below 10 having a prefixed 0 for symmetry; each number is separated from the next by a hyphen, and the divider, which distinguishes the words in the original, is represented by the spacing of the words. Thus the words for 'girl' and 'boy' mentioned above (p. 34) will be spelt 70-54 and 70-42. Ventris did in fact begin with an alphabetic system, but this is rather confusing and he himself ended by abandoning it. For the benefit of those who prefer the signs, some of the principal words on which the 'grid' was built are illustrated in Fig. 12.

It must be emphasized that Ventris remained in favour of Etruscan connexions for Minoan right up to the middle of 1952. The Work Notes are full of comparisons with Etruscan and attempts at relating the Minoan to Etruscan words and suffixes. But this did not hinder his methodical analysis and his attempts to wrest the meaning from the texts by purely combinatory methods. In this period he kept up a fruitful correspondence with Bennett,

Children

70 54 70 42

Spelling variations

38	03	31	06	37		28	03	31	06	37
08	27	03	20	61		08	27	11	20	61

Links

28	38
03	11
38	46
44	70
14	42	51
60	76
44	74

Inflexion

Nominative	'Genitive'	'Prepositional' (‡ +)
		03 02

Nominative				'Genitive'					'Prepositional'				
08	39	32	59	08	39	32	59	61					
54	06	59	36	54	06	59	36	36	54	06	59	36	
11	02	10	04	11	02	10	04	42	11	02	10	04	75
10													

Consonant links

					Masculine	Feminine
02	60				02	60
05	37				12	
06	30	52			31	
10	40	42	54	75	36	57
12	31	41			42	54
32	78					
36	46					
38	28					
44	70					
53	76					

Fig. 12. The building of the grid.

who had written a dissertation on the Pylos tablets in 1947, though this was never seen by Ventris. Other scholars, too, contributed to the exchange of views, notably the Greek K. D. Ktistopoulos.

Little real progress could be made until the publication in 1951 of Bennett's *The Pylos Tablets*, a transcript of the tablets found in 1939. This for the first time contained reliable lists of the signs; hitherto there had been much confusion of similar signs. The first task was the compilation of statistical tables showing the over-all frequency of each sign, and its frequency in initial, final and other positions in the sign groups. Simultaneously with Ventris similar tables were prepared by Bennett and Ktistopoulos. This in itself made certain conclusions possible. Three signs predominated at the beginning of words: 08, Evans' 'double-axe' sign; 61, Evans' 'throne-and-sceptre' sign; and 38. 61 was not uncommon also as a final sign; the other two occurred rarely elsewhere; but it was clear that all three could stand inside a word. The theory that they were determinatives, or classifying signs not meant to be pronounced, was thus, if not disproved, made less likely, since it would be necessary to postulate two uses of the same sign in word groups: a determinative use at the beginning of the word, and a syllabic value in other positions. But reflexion on syllabic writing suggested a much easier solution. If words are written in a syllabary which has signs only for pure vowels and for consonants followed by vowels, then a vowel sign will only be used in the middle of a word if it immediately follows another vowel; but all words beginning with a vowel must start with a vowel sign. To take an example in English, *individual* will have to be written, with extra vowels, *i-n(i)-di-vi-du-a-l(a)*. It does not matter what the language is; if it is written in this way, the analysis of the use of the signs will show a characteristic pattern of distribution: the plain vowels occur rarely in the middle of a word (like *a* in *individual*), but frequently at the beginning, because every word beginning with a vowel must begin with a vowel sign. In the middle of a word most vowels are preceded by a consonant, and will therefore be written with a compound sign for consonant plus vowel. A check against the Cypriot inscriptions written in the syllabic script shows this clearly; both *a* and *e* have precisely this distribution. The other vowels do not show it so clearly, because the Greek language employs them commonly in diphthongs or after other vowels. It was therefore possible to deduce that these three signs, 08, 61 and 38, or at least 08 and 38, were plain vowels.

Another deduction sprang from the observation that 78 was a common final sign. Take, for example, this heading to a list of weighed quantities of some substance:

```
36-14-12-41   70-27-04-27   51-80-04-78
11-02-70-27-04-27-78   77-60-40-11-02-78   61-39-58-70-78
      61-39-77-72-38-75-78
77-70   06-40-36   03-59-36-28-78   38-44-41-78   43-77-31-80
```

From this and a number of similar texts Ventris deduced that 78 was a conjunction, probably meaning 'and' and attached to the end of the word it served to connect (like *-que* in Latin), thus:

> - - - A and B
> and C and D and E and F
> - - - - - - and X and Y - - -

The fact that it was not an essential part of the word, but a separable suffix, emerged clearly from the comparison of similar words, as 70-27-04-27 in the first line and (11-02-)70-27-04-27(-78) in the second; just as in English adverbs are distinguished from adjectives by having the suffix *-ly* tacked on to them. Some prefixes also could be identified by similar means; 61-, occasionally alternating with 36-; 61-39-; and in a special case 08-.

Another useful line of approach was offered by certain words which appeared in two different spellings. In some cases it was not easy to be sure that these were not two different words; but if they were long enough, but differed in only one syllable, then it was a reasonable assumption that they had something in common, especially if they were in like contexts. For instance, a word already believed to be a personal name occurred in identical formulas, once spelt 38-03-31-06-37, and once with the initial 38 corrected by the scribe into 28. It is a happy feature of the tablets that erased signs can often be read despite the erasure; the clay still bears traces of the original reading, even when another sign has been written over it. This suggests that there is a connexion between 38 and 28. Similarly, 08-27-03-20-61 respelt 08-27-11-20-61 suggests that 03 is related to 11, and this link is confirmed elsewhere. Parallel examples give us, less certainly, 38 related to 46, 44 to 70, 14 to 42 and 51, 60 to 76, 44 to 74. Mere errors may be misleading, but they can also be revealing. When I use a typewriter, never having been taught to type, I often press one key instead of the next; if a large enough number of examples were collected and analysed, it would be possible to observe that I often type *w* or *r* in place of *e*, but rarely other letters. From this it might be deduced that the keys *w e r* came together, and so eventually the whole keyboard might be reconstructed. In writing the factors are more complicated, but usually one letter or group of letters is substituted for another of similar sound. Thus if *attention* is written *atenshun*, we can deduce that *t* and *tt* are alike, and that *tio* sounds something like *shu*. In the case of a syllabic script, the link may be either in the vowel or in the consonant; for instance, the pairs may be related as *do* to *to* or as *do* to *du*.

The greatest number of variations in words, however, was to be found in their endings. Miss Kober had already found some examples and suggested that they represented inflexions, that is, modifications of the ending of the word to denote grammatical relationship; as, for instance, in English *boxes* and *boxing* might be recognized as inflected forms of the simple word *box*. Fortunately lists such as the tablets contain consist almost entirely of nouns, so that the problems of inflexions in the verb could at this stage be left aside, and almost all variations explained as inflexions in the declension of nouns. With the new material Ventris was able to go far beyond her observations and distinguish various types of inflexion. In some cases these consisted in adding an extra sign: thus 08-39-32-59 forms another case (already tentatively labelled 'genitive') by adding -61. Other nouns form a similar case by adding -36. In another type, however, inflexion causes the ending of the ordinary ('nominative') case to be replaced by other signs in the other cases: thus 11-02-10-04-10 has its 'genitive' 11-02-10-04-42 and another case (that following the word 03-02) 11-02-10-04-75. These cases were tentatively identified by the study of certain words, believed to be proper names, which changed in each line of a certain class of tablet, though the formula in the rest of the line remained the same. When these names reappeared in other formulas, then they took the variant forms identified as inflected cases. The word 03-02 occurred frequently before such names, and was always followed by a particular form of the name.

Now these variations might be due to adding unrelated suffixes, like the Japanese 'postpositions' which behave much as inflected endings: 'nominative' *hito-ha*, 'genitive' *hito-no*, 'accusative' *hito-wo*. But if it is a true inflexion, it is more likely to follow the pattern of Latin: *domin-us, domin-i, domin-o*. The Japanese *hito* is an independent word which can stand alone; but in Latin there is no independent *domin*—it must be completed by the grammatical ending. If the Latin forms are written in a syllabic script, the termination will in fact represent -*nus*, -*ni*, -*no*, that is to say the consonant of the alternating suffixes, being part of the stem, remains unchanged. The existence of a number of different types of inflexion pointed to the second possibility; in Japanese all nouns show the same limited set of suffixes, and there is no true inflexion.

By this means it was possible to establish a fresh series of links between signs which could be suspected of containing the same consonant but different vowels. The final signs of the declension given above, 10 replaced by 42 or 75, will form a group of this type. Ventris in August 1951 prepared a list of 159 words from the Pylos tablets which showed what he took to be inflexional varia-

tion; and from this and other lists of Knossos words he derived
a large number of possible links between signs sharing the same
consonant. Not all of these could be right, he pointed out, but
those which occurred several times in different words were at
least likely. The probable ones are worth tabulating here; where
more than two signs are involved, this is generally based on a
combination of several equations.

02	60			
05	37			
06	30	52		
10	40	42	54	75
12	31	41		
32	78			
36	46			
38	28			
44	70			
53	76			

In some cases the inflexional variation seemed to be due to a
change of gender rather than case; this could be seen from the use
of these words with the ideograms for men and women. Thus
Ventris was able to list:

MASCULINE	FEMININE
02	60
12	31
36	57
42	54

He considered the third of these doubtful, since he was for other
reasons inclined to regard the derivatives formed with -57 as
plurals. This gender table suggested a further series of links, which
Ventris worked on in September 1951. If the masculines all form
their feminines alike, as in Latin

MASCULINE	FEMININE
domin-us	*domin-a*
bon-us	*bon-a*
serv-us	*serv-a*

then we may deduce that the two columns (02 12 36 42 and 60 31 57 54) each form a series sharing the same vowel, but with different consonants. At this stage it was difficult to judge which of the links so found were correct, but Ventris built up a table showing which were the most probable and consistent. The signs were allotted to columns according to the function of the suffix. Not only masculine and feminine, but the other recognizable cases and derivatives each had a column, thus allowing the principle of links between signs having the same vowel to be extended.

'We may in this way', wrote Ventris in Work Note 15 of 3 September 1951, 'be able to construct a second dimension to our "GRID" which will make it the skeleton of a true table of phonetic values. It will then only need the identification of a small number of syllabic values for the more or less complete system of consonants and vowels to fit into place. Though it would evidently be better to wait until the "GRID" can be further corrected by the full Knossos evidence, it is conceivable that some happy accident or intuition might lead to such a solution at any time now.' Clearly Ventris felt that the solution was not far off; but he was still convinced that the language would prove to be of the little known pre-Greek type, to which Etruscan afforded the only clue, and that a poor one.

The next stage was to construct from this table a rough syllabic grid, using as many of the equations as seemed to be consistent and valid. The result was to bring together the different types of linkage found, so that the vowel columns could be reduced to five, and the consonant lines to fifteen. The diagram, reproduced as Fig. 13, is dated Athens, 28 September 1951. A check with the values as established later will show up a number of errors; but already the main lines were emerging. The grid is given below in the numerical form; signs in brackets are those regarded as doubtful and these were drawn on a smaller scale in Ventris' original.

Vowels ...	I	II	III	IV	V
Pure vowels?	61	—	—	—	08
Semi-vowel?	—	—	—	59	57
Consonant I	40	10	75	42	54
II	39	11	—	—	03
III	—	(14)	—	51	01
IV	37	05	—	—	66
V	41	12	—	55	31
VI	30	52	—	24	06
VII	46	36	—	—	—
VIII	73	15	—	(72)	80
IX	—	70	—	44	(74)
X	53	—	(04)	76	20
XI	60	02	27	26	33
XII	28	—	—	38	77
XIII	—	32	78	—	—
XIV	07	—	—	—	—
XV	67	—	—	—	—

In November Ventris corrected this table by studying the words ending in the nominative in -10; he had noticed that they all declined alike, changing -10 to -42 in the 'genitive' and to -75 in the 'prepositional' case (after 03-02). This led him to a new theory; there were certain limits to the signs which could appear immediately before this termination. This would be most easily explained if the termination was always preceded by the same vowel, so that here was another means of building up a new series of signs with different consonants but the same vowel. He now reconstructed vowel III as follows:

Consonant I	75	XI	27
V	55	XII	38
VI	24	XIII	78
VIII	72	?	13
IX	44	?	09
X	04		

This was an excellent move; in fact only one sign (55) was wrongly placed. It was now time, Ventris went on, to cast about

LINEAR SCRIPT B SYLLABIC GRID
(2ND STATE)

DIAGNOSIS OF CONSONANT AND VOWEL EQUATIONS IN THE INFLEXIONAL MATERIAL FROM PYLOS: ATHENS, 28 SEPT 51

THESE 51 SIGNS MAKE UP 90% OF ALL SIGN-OCCURRENCES IN THE PYLOS SIGNGROUP INDEX. APPENDED FIGURES GIVE EACH SIGN'S OVERALL FREQUENCY PER MILLE IN THE PYLOS INDEX.

	Impure ending - typical syllables before -? & -☐ in Case 2c & 3	Pure ending, typical nominatives of forms in Column I	Includes possible "accusatives"	Also, but less frequently, the nominatives of forms in Column I	
	THESE SIGNS DON'T OCCUR BEFORE -☐-	THESE SIGNS OCCUR LESS COMMONLY OR NOT AT ALL BEFORE -☐-			
	MORE OFTEN FEMININE THAN MASCULINE?	MORE OFTEN MASCULINE THAN FEMININE?			MORE OFTEN FEMININE THAN MASCULINE?
	NORMALLY FORM THE GENITIVE SINGULAR BY ADDING -?		NORMALLY FORM THE GENITIVE SINGULAR BY ADDING -☐		
	vowel 1	vowel 2	vowel 3	vowel 4	vowel 5
pure vowels?	30.5				37.2
a semi-vowel?				34.0	29.4
consonant 1	14.8	32.5	21.2	28.1	18.8
2	19.6	17.5			13.7
3		9.2		3.3	10.0
4	17.0	28.6			0.4
5	17.7	10.3		4.1	10.2
6	7.4	20.5		14.8	14.4
7	4.1	44.0			
8	6.1	6.1		13.5	15.2
9		33.1		32.3	2.4
10	22.2		34.8	3.5	2.2
11	31.2	33.8	34.4	8.3	0.7
12	17.0			37.7	24.0
13		9.4	14.2		
14	5.0				
15	12.6				

MICHAEL VENTRIS

Fig. 13. Ventris' 'grid', 28 September 1951.

for a similar suffix in words or names borrowed by Greek from a pre-Greek source. He added significantly: 'The latter [Greek forms] are also worth considering on the remoter possibility that the Knossos and Pylos tablets are actually written in Greek, though I feel that what we have so far seen of Minoan forms makes this unlikely.'

It was of course impossible to reconcile the Minoan inflexions with Greek ones on the assumption that the spelling rules of Cypriot held good for Linear B too. Ventris therefore went on to explore possible equivalents among Etruscan noun suffixes, without much success; but at one point he remarked: 'The Greek masculine ending *-eus*, whether or not it is connected, is an almost perfect equivalent of the function which I read into the Minoan -10.' Here, though he did not realize it, he had grasped the truth; but there was still a long way to go.

Further work on a variety of topics during the winter of 1951-2 led to small advances in the general understanding of the nature of the texts and various minor points of inflexion. For instance, a mysterious, but common, ideogram had been previously discussed on the theory that it represented flax, because in some forms it looked vaguely like a ball of thread on a spindle. This Ventris now, quite rightly, abandoned, and concluded that it meant a commodity of some kind which could be used in the payment of wages. He did indeed hint at the meaning 'grain', which we now feel certain is the correct value, in all probability, 'wheat'. By February, when the publication of the full Knossos texts in *Scripta Minoa II* was imminent, Ventris was ready with a modified grid. The second line (semi-vowel) was now simply numbered consonant I, so there is a consequent change in the other numbers. The signs in brackets represent doubtful or alternative placings. Some very tentative identifications were proposed for the vowels and consonants; they were derived largely from Ventris' attempts at providing Etruscan parallels, and took little account of the Cypriot syllabary. In fact all four vowels were right; of the horizontal lines the following were correct or nearly so: the pure vowels, III = p (given as an alternative), V and VI both = t (in fact V = d, VI = t), VIII = n, XI = r or l, XII = l. But the relative placing of the signs was much better than the identifications.

Vowels ...	I = -i?	II = -o?	III = -e?	IV	V = -a?	Un-certain
Pure vowels?	61	—	—	—	08	—
Consonant I	—	—	59	—	57	—
II	40	10	75	42	54	—
III	39	—	(39)	—	03	11
IV	46	36	(46)	—	(57)	—
V	—	14	—	—	01, 51	—
VI	37	05	(04)	—	—	66
VII	41	12	55	—	31	—
VIII	30	52	24	—	06	—
IX	73	15	(72)	—	80	—
X	—	70	44, (74)	—	(20)	(45)
XI	53	—	(04)	—	76	(20)
XII	60	02	27	—	26	33
XIII	28	—	38	—	(77)	—
XIV	—	—	13	—	—	—
XV	—	32	78	—	(32)	58
Other con-sonants	(67, 07)	—	(09, 45)	—	—	—

Work Note 19 (20 March 1952) now makes disappointing reading. Ventris had made considerable progress in reconstructing the inflexional system of the language, and this note was intended to clear up one detail of that system. It is devoted to a study of the suffix -41, which Ventris correctly identified as in some cases denoting an 'oblique' case of the plural. (We now know that it is -*si*, the termination of the dative plural of a large group of nouns in Greek; but it is also common as a verb ending, and it occurs in other circumstances too, owing to the spelling rules; the group thus studied was therefore not homogeneous.) Much space was given to the search for Etruscan parallels, which of course proved vain.

Work Note 20 (1 June 1952) was introduced by its author as 'a frivolous digression' and was headed: 'Are the Knossos and Pylos tablets written in Greek?' *Scripta Minoa II* was now available, but no one, not even Ventris, had yet made a full analysis. Ventris was well aware that he was flying in the face of expert opinion in daring to consider the possibility of Greeks at Knossos in the fifteenth century B.C. Hence the rather casual way in which he treated this theory, which he expected shortly to disprove.

However, he did not start with the Greek hypothesis and see if it would fit. The title was a description added after the work had been done, for the starting-point was deliberately chosen to be independent of the Greek language. This was the group of words which Ventris had classified as 'Category 3', and they included Miss Kober's 'triplets', which we met in the last chapter. The key supposition was that these were place-names, a step Miss Kober had not taken. Ventris analysed them as follows:

They are sign-groups which are not personal names, and yet figure as the subjects of very varied lists of commodities, often recurring in a fixed order.... Their commonest members are formed, in each case [i.e. at both Knossos and Pylos], by a group of about a dozen...which are found in a disproportionately large number of entries.

From the analogy of the contemporary accounts from Ras Shamra/ Ugarit...which should be one of our most valuable aids, I think it is likely that the Category 3 sign-groups correspond to the *'towns and corporations'* of Ugarit....Those which occur *both* at Pylos and at Knossos are probably 'corporations'; those which are peculiar to each are the 'towns' and villages of the region, the adjectival forms in -37/-57 being their ethnica.

That is to say, the longer forms would be the adjectives (masculine and feminine) derived from the names of the towns, like *Athens/ Athenian*. The Knossos names offered some hope of identification with names surviving into the classical period.

To this three phonetic suggestions were added: that $08 = a$ because of its great initial frequency; that consonant VIII was *n-*, because Cypriot *na*[1] is identifiable with 06; that vowel I was -*i*, because Cypriot *ti*[1] is almost identical with 37, and this vowel is common before 57 (=*ja*?) but never occurs before 61 (=*i*?). This last is the only mistake; 61 = *o*.

A name which is likely to occur at Knossos is that of the nearby harbour town, Amnisos, mentioned by Homer. The consonant group -*mn*- will have to be spelled out by inserting an extra vowel, since every consonant must be followed by a vowel. It should therefore have the form approximately *a-mi-ni-so*, or using the clues we have 08-..-30-... We find in the tablets one suitable word, and only one, containing these signs. It occurs in the following forms:

> 08-73-30-12 (simple form)
> 08-73-30-41-36⎫
> 08-73-30-41-57⎭ (adjectival forms)
> 08-73-30-12-45 ('locative' form?)

Since 73 and 30 both have the same vowel, as we see from their placing in column I of the grid, this confirms our guess that an extra vowel will be inserted of the same sort as the following real vowel: -*m*[i]-*ni*- will stand for -*mni*-. This exactly matches the Cypriot convention. Sign 12 is therefore perhaps *so*, and all the names ending in -12 will represent the common Greek types ending in -*sos* or -*ssos*. This confirms the suggestion that vowel II is -*o*. The other very common name is 70-52-12, which we can now decode as: .*o-no-so*. It is not difficult to guess that the first vowel here is another extra, and the consonant must be *k*, giving *ko-no-so* as a plausible spelling for *Knōssos*. The third name in -12 is 69-53-12 = ..-.*i-so*, which Ventris conjectured might be *tu-li-so* = *Tulissos*, another important town in Central Crete; but he cautiously characterized this as less certain. 69 was a relatively rare sign, which had not been placed on the grid.

He then turned to the name of a commodity, found at Knossos

---

[1] See Fig. 7, p. 24.

and Pylos with variant spellings, but attached to the same ideogram (rather like a mug with a lid on it) and in similar contexts:

Knossos   70-53-57-14-52
Pylos   70-53-25-01-06

The grid shows that the endings in each form have the same vowel: 14 and 52 are both in column II, 01 and 06 both in column V; and the identity of the two words is clear from the fact that the consonants are the same: 14 and 01 are both on line V, 52 and 06 both on line VIII. The ending may then be written as -*t°-no*, -*tª-na*, and the whole word now comes out as *ko-l/ri-ja-t°-no* (*j* is to be understood as a semi-vowel like the English *y*). This strongly suggests the Greek word *koriannon* or *koliandron*, the spice 'coriander'. This, however, though known to us as a Greek word, is probably in origin borrowed from some other language, so that its presence in Minoan does not necessarily imply that Minoan is Greek.

Ventris then reverted to the adjectival forms of the place-names, which now appear as, for example, *a-mi-ni-si-jo* (masculine) and *a-mi-ni-si-ja* (feminine). He acutely observed that if we suppose that final -*s*, -*n* and -*i* after another vowel are omitted, these forms are precisely the Greek derivative forms: masculine *Amnisios* (or plural *Amnisioi*), feminine *Amnisia* (or plural *Amnisiai*). The puzzling genitive ending -36-36 will be -*jo-jo* agreeing with the archaic Greek genitives in -(*i*)-*oio*. The other genitive ending -61 appeared as a difficulty, since the feminine declension with nominative in -*ā*, genitive -*ās*, would show no variation in spelling if the final -*s* were omitted, as he suspected; and he noted that the genitive of 28-46-27-57 (ending -*ja*) is actually the same as the nominative.

Turning next to the words for 'boys' and 'girls', 70-42 and 70-54, both began with *ko*-. Now there are a number of words for 'boy' in Greek, but only one which begins with *ko*- (or *kho*- or *go*-, which on the analogy of Cypriot are also possible interpretations of the sign *ko*). This is the classical (Attic) Greek *koros*, with a feminine form for 'girl', *korē*. Here for the first time we must face a linguistic problem. Classical Greek is in general the dialect of Attica, the speech of Athens; but we know from inscriptions and some literary texts a great many other dialects, which are equally Greek, but differ in their forms from Attic. Now Homer, who writes mainly in Ionic, has the word for 'boy' in the form *kouros*; and the Doric dialects make it generally into *kōros*. From these variant forms it is possible to deduce that the original form, from which all these dialect variations came, was *korwos*; and confirmation of this comes from the Arcadian dialect, which actually preserves a feminine form *korwā*. This is the origin of Attic *korē*, since Attic not only loses the *w*, but changes *ā* into *ē* (pronounced rather like *ay* in *bay*, but with a pure vowel and rather broader). Thus if we are looking for a primitive form of Greek we shall expect these words to appear as *korwos*, *korwā*. Ventris saw that 70-42 and 70-54 would fit, 'provided we assume some abbreviation in the spelling', as *ko(r)-wo(s)*, plural *ko(r)-wo(i)*, and *ko(r)-wā*, plural *ko(r)-wa(i)*. The assumption of an 'abbreviation' of this sort was daring; but the possibility was worth testing. Consonant II in the grid would then be *w*; and it is clear that something has gone wrong with this line, for 42 must displace 10 in column II. But the correction is now automatic. The declension -10, -42, -75, which is preceded by a column III (*e*?) vowel, now appears as -*e*-.., -*e-wo*, -*e-we*. This at once recalls the Greek declension in -*eus* (so that 10 will be *u*), with its archaic genitive -*ēwos*. The 'prepositional' case appears not to fit exactly, for we should expect -*e-wi*; but Ventris thought of a locative (a case not surviving in Classical Greek), -*ēwe*.

The word for 'total', 05-12, 05-31, can now be transcribed *to-so*, *to-sa* and interpreted as *to(s)-so(s)* or *to(s)-so(n)* 'so much' (masculine and neuter), or *to(s)-so(i)* 'so many' (masculine); and *to(s)-sā* 'so much' (feminine), or *to(s)-sa(i)*, *to(s)-sa* 'so many' (feminine and neuter). Sign 45, doubtfully placed on the grid, was now tried with the value *te* (also *the*, *de*), so that the longer form of the totalling formula 05-12-45 becomes *to(s)-so(n)-de*, etc.; and the same suffix applied to place-names will give, for example, *Amniso(n)-de* 'to Amnisos' or *Amniso-the(n)* 'from Amnisos' or possibly even *Amniso-thi* 'at Amnisos'.

Some words from the Knossos chariot tablets also suggested Greek: 08-60-02-15-04-13-06 can be transcribed *a-l/r.-l/r.-m.-t.-.....* This beginning recalls the Greek word *(h)armata,* 'chariots'; but although Ventris had identified -13-06 as a verbal ending, he did not yet see that it was the termination of the passive participle *-mena.* But 'the Greek chimera', wrote Ventris, 'again raises its head' in the phrase 08-60-26-57 08-30-57-39 *a-ra-ru-ja (h)ā-ni-jā-phi,* which is recognizable as meaning 'fitted with reins'; the Attic form would be *araruiai hēniais,* but the ending *-phi* is common in Homer, and the form is quite acceptable.

Ventris ended this Note with a warning: 'If pursued, I suspect that this line of decipherment would sooner or later come to an impasse, or dissipate itself in absurdities.' He called attention to features which appeared not to fit Greek; for instance, the conjunction -78, which it seemed impossible to equate with the appropriate Greek word *te,* 'and'. Here Ventris failed to reckon with the archaism of the language which he was dealing with.

But even while this Note was in the post, on its way to scholars all over the world, Ventris did pursue this lead, and found to his astonishment that the Greek solution was inescapable. Slowly and painfully the mute signs were being forced to speak, and what they spoke was Greek—mangled and truncated it is true, but recognizable none the less as the Greek language.

CHAPTER 5

GROWTH AND DEVELOPMENT

Cryptography is a science of deduction and controlled experiment; hypotheses are formed, tested and often discarded. But the residue which passes the test grows and grows until finally there comes a point when the experimenter feels solid ground beneath his feet: his hypotheses cohere, and fragments of sense emerge from their camouflage. The code 'breaks'. Perhaps this is best defined as the point when the likely leads appear faster than they can be followed up. It is like the initiation of a chain-reaction in atomic physics; once the critical threshold is passed, the reaction propagates itself. Only in the simplest experiments or codes does it complete itself with explosive violence. In the more difficult cases there is much work still to be done, and the small areas of sense, though sure proof of the break, remain for a while isolated; only gradually does the picture become filled out.

In June 1952 Ventris felt that the Linear B script had broken. Admittedly the tentative Greek words suggested in Work Note 20 were too few to carry conviction; in particular they implied an unlikely set of spelling conventions. But as he transcribed more and more texts, so the Greek words began to emerge in greater numbers; new signs could now be identified by recognizing a word in which one sign only was a blank, and this value could then be tested elsewhere. The spelling rules received confirmation, and the pattern of the decipherment became clear.

It so happened that at this moment Ventris was asked by the B.B.C. to give a talk on the Third Programme in connexion with the publication of *Scripta Minoa II*. He determined to take this opportunity of bringing his discovery before the public. He gave first a brief historical account of the script and its discovery, and then proceeded to outline his method. Finally came the astonishing announcement:

> During the last few weeks, I have come to the conclusion that the Knossos and Pylos tablets must, after all, be written in Greek—a difficult and archaic Greek, seeing that it is 500 years older than Homer and written in a rather abbreviated form, but Greek nevertheless.
>
> Once I made this assumption, most of the peculiarities of the language and spelling which had puzzled me seemed to find a logical explanation; and although many of the tablets remain as incomprehensible as before, many others are suddenly beginning to make sense.[1]

He went on to quote four well known Greek words which he claimed to have found (*poimēn*, 'shepherd', *kerameus*, 'potter', *khalkeus*, 'bronze-smith', *khrusoworgos*, 'gold-smith'), and to translate eight phrases. He ended on a suitably cautious note: 'I have suggested that there is now a better chance of reading these earliest European inscriptions than ever before, but there is evidently a great deal more work to do before we are all agreed on the solution of the problem.'

I do not think it can be said that this broadcast made a great impression; but I for one was an eager listener. In view of the recurrent claims that had been made, I did not regard Ventris' system as standing much chance; in particular I already had a pretty clear notion what Mycenaean Greek should look like, and I doubted whether Ventris had. The word *khrusoworgos*, however, was encouraging; *w* did not exist in most forms of Greek of the classical period, but should certainly appear in an archaic dialect, since its loss, as in Homer, was known to be recent. But the principles outlined by Ventris were in close agreement with those I had formulated for myself; if correctly followed the results might well be right. And I was not, as most of the archaeologists were, prejudiced against the Greek solution; six years before I had tried to test the few available Pylos texts on that assumption, but the material was too scanty. I must confess that in 1952 I was ill prepared; shortly before that I had been appointed to a post at

[1] *The Listener*, 10 July 1952.

Cambridge, and all my spare time was devoted to writing lectures for the following October.

The claim of Ventris, however, was too important and too relevant to my subject, the Greek dialects, to be overlooked. The first thing was to see Sir John Myres and ask his opinion, for I knew he was in touch with Ventris. He sat as usual in his canvas chair at a great desk, his legs wrapped in a rug. He was too infirm to move much, and he motioned me to a chair. 'Mm, Ventris', he said in answer to my question, 'he's a young architect.' As Myres at that time was himself eighty-two, I wondered if 'young' meant less than sixty. 'Here's his stuff', he went on, 'I don't know what to make of it. I'm not a philologist.' On the whole he appeared sceptical, though admitting that he had not sufficient specialized knowledge to judge if the proposed Greek was sound. But he had some of Ventris' notes, including the latest version of the grid, which he let me copy, promising at the same time to put me in direct contact with Ventris.

I went home eager to try out the new theory. I approached the matter very cautiously, for impressed as I had been by the broadcast, I had a horrid feeling the Greek would turn out to be only vague resemblances to Greek words, as in Georgiev's 'decipherment', and wrong for the sort of dialect we expected. I set to work transcribing words from the two sets of texts, and in four days I had convinced myself that the identifications were in the main sound. I collected a list of twenty-three plausible Greek words I had found in the tablets, some of which had not then been noted by Ventris, and on 9 July I wrote to Myres stating my conclusion. I wrote, too, to Ventris, congratulating him on having found the solution, and putting forward a number of new suggestions.

His reply (13 July) was typically frank and modest. 'At the moment', he wrote, 'I feel rather in need of moral support.... I'm conscious that there's a *lot* which so far can't be very satisfactorily explained.' I had tentatively asked if I could be any help to him; he replied: 'I've been feeling the need of a "mere philologist" to keep me on the right lines....It would be extremely useful to me if I could count on your help, not only in trying to make sense out of the material, but also in drawing the correct conclusions about the formations in terms of dialect and stage of development.' Thus was formed a partnership which was to last more than four years.

A further sentence of this letter must be quoted for it introduces a crucial point. 'I'm glad we coincided in some of the values which occurred to me after I wrote to Myres, though I suppose a court of law might suppose I'd pre-cooked the material in such a way that the coincidence wasn't conclusive.' If we had both suggested the same values independently, only two conclusions were possible: that they were right and the decipherment was therefore proved; or that Ventris had deliberately planted the evidence for others to find. One had only to make Ventris' acquaintance to realize that the latter alternative was out of the question. Thus at the outset I felt absolutely sure that the foundation had been truly laid, whatever difficulties remained; and nothing since has shaken my faith in the least. Ventris himself had attacks of cold feet that summer; for instance he wrote on 28 July: 'Every other day I get so doubtful about the whole thing that I'd almost rather it was someone else's.' He was worried over some discrepancies between Mycenaean and classical Greek; on some of these points I was able to set his mind at rest. For instance, there was no reason to be bothered by the absence of the definite article; philologists had anticipated its absence in the early-stages of the language. This phase of our co-operation did not last long, for in an amazingly short time Ventris had mastered the details of Greek philology for himself.

One of my early suggestions was the value *nu* for sign no. 55. I had noted that it gave some good words, and in particular the divine name *Enualios* in company with Athena and Poseidon. Ventris wrote back: 'I've a rooted objection to finding gods' names on the tablets...but *Athana potnia* [mistress Athena] certainly looks too good to be true.'

The first thing Ventris did was to draw up a list of words for which plausible Greek equivalents could be suggested. He called it an 'Experimental Vocabulary' and it contained 553 entries (including proper names); a very few of these we now recognize to be wrong, a few more have been modified, but in the main the Greek words here provided a sound foundation on which we could build. There remained still a number of the rarer signs whose values were not yet established, and the texts that were completely intelligible were few. But already we could read:

PU-RO *i-je-re-ja do-e-ra e-ne-ka ku-ru-so-jo i-je-ro-jo* WOMEN 14
ΠΥΛΟΣ· ἱερείας δοῦλαι ἕνεκα χρυσοῖο ἱεροῖο

At Pylos: slaves of the priestess on account of sacred gold: 14 women.

This tablet illustrates clearly two other points. First, the word *e-ne-ka* was puzzling, because although it agreed exactly with the classical Greek word *heneka* ('on account of'), the etymologists had conjectured that the earlier form was *henweka*, which would demand the Mycenaean spelling *e-nu-we-ka*. However, the word occurs several times, so there is no question of an error. One is driven to suppose either that the etymologists were wrong, or that there is some special reason why the *w* was lost in the Mycenaean form.

Secondly, the mere fact of being able to translate the tablet does not automatically answer all the questions. Why were these women slaves of the priestess? Which priestess? What was the sacred gold? What was the state of affairs or the transaction that this tablet was meant to record? All these are questions which we cannot answer; the facts were known to the writer of the tablet, and he did not expect it to be read by anyone who did not have the same knowledge; just as many of us make jottings in our diaries which convey a clear message to us, but would be meaningless to a stranger ignorant of the circumstances in which they were written. This problem is still with us, and will always remain; we cannot know all the facts and events of which the tablets are an only partial record. We have to examine them as minutely as we can, to compare them with similar documents elsewhere, to check them against the archaeological evidence. Imagination may help to fill in the gaps, and in chapter 7 I shall attempt to look beyond the texts at life in the Mycenaean world; but it is no good pretending we know more than we do.

My correspondence with Ventris developed into a rapid exchange of views, and although we met from time to time to discuss problems and plan our work, most of it was done alone and then submitted to the other for criticism. We followed this method in our joint publications; each drafted sections, which the other then criticized, and the whole was often rewritten to take account of objections raised. This method could never have worked, had we not been so much in harmony in our general attitude to the problem. We had many differences, but they were never serious, and most were resolved before we put anything into print; and the advantage of having everything checked by a second person in no small measure contributed to our confidence in our joint work.

The first project was a full length technical article on the decipherment, and I was flattered when Ventris asked me to contribute to it. I had no wish to take more than the small share of credit due to me, but he was anxious that it should be published jointly; my suggestions could in this way be incorporated without detailed acknowledgement, and, more important, joint authorship was some guarantee that it was at the least a shared delusion.

The title was carefully chosen to avoid extravagant claims: 'Evidence for Greek Dialect in the Mycenaean Archives'. We did not claim to have deciphered Linear B; we presented some evidence which we had found. 'Dialect' was used rather than 'language' in order to emphasize that we recognized a new dialect of Greek, and 'archives' served to show that we had no illusions about the type of document we were trying to read. The most daring choice was the use of 'Mycenaean' rather than Linear B; it was our intention to state plainly a fact boggled at or side-stepped by almost all who had written on the subject. The label 'Minoan' had been out of date as far as Linear B was concerned since 1939; the usual remedy was to ignore the fact that Pylos was a Mycenaean, not a Minoan site; or to camouflage the difficulty under a hybrid name like Minoan–Mycenaean or Creto–Mycenaean. With our conviction that Linear B contained Greek went the irresistible conclusion that Knossos in the Late Minoan II period formed part of the Mycenaean world. This is perhaps what, more than anything else, stuck in the throats of the archaeologists. But the insistence was justified, and the name Mycenaean, originally a label for the culture of the Greek mainland in the Late Helladic period, is now generally extended to the Linear B script and the dialect it contains. The discovery of Linear B tablets at Mycenae in 1952 gave additional weight to this choice of name.

The writing and rewriting of 'Evidence', as this article has come to be called, took until November of 1952. We were lucky enough, through the kind offices of Mr T. J. Dunbabin, to get it accepted for publication in the 1953 issue of the *Journal of Hellenic Studies*—lucky for two reasons: it is still difficult to get an article into print in a British classical journal in less than eighteen months, and in 1952 the aftermath of the war added to the delays of publication; and an article of this kind was exceedingly hard for the editors to appraise. If it proved yet another damp squib it would be unfortunate to have wasted twenty pages of valuable space on it; on the other hand, if the authors were justified in their claim, it was of first-rate importance, and would be a credit to the journal which published it. Fortunately the editors decided to publish. For this we were thankful; otherwise we should have been forced to publish it abroad—Professor Björck had already offered space in the Swedish journal *Eranos* for it.

The first section of the article advanced the proposition that Linear B contained Greek as a reasonable historical hypothesis.

Next came an analysis of the texts entirely on internal evidence, explaining very briefly the principles of the syllabic grid. This part has been misunderstood and misinterpreted by our critics, and even our supporters have complained of its inadequacy. But considerations of space precluded the step-by-step analysis which had occupied so many pages of the Work Notes, and once the solution had been achieved it seemed more important to assemble the complete evidence for how it worked than the partial clues which had led to it. Perhaps this was an error of judgement on our part; but we should have found editors less accommodating if we had spread ourselves here.

One of the difficulties which besets everyone who writes on this subject is that of printing. It was necessary to quote numerous words and phrases in Linear B, and to have inserted specially made blocks for each word would have made the cost prohibitive. Instead we quoted words in our own transcription, a table of which was printed; but this was helped out by another page of 223 words and phrases in Linear B, numbered for reference in the text. This expedient saved money, but led to a somewhat confusing anticipation of the results.

The experimental syllabic grid gave values for sixty-five signs, seven of which were shown as tentative. Subsequent work has removed most of the queries, but one sign was completely wrong (qo_2 is now known to be *su*), and some minor modifications have been made (da_2 is now generally regarded as *du*, and nu_2 is more precisely *nwa*). But the vast majority of these values have never been questioned, except by those who reject the decipherment entirely. It is a case of all or nothing.

We then put forward the 'assumed rules of Mycenaean orthography'. These rules had been forced upon us as the result of identifying the Mycenaean words as Greek; they were in many respects unexpected and unwelcome; but it needs to be emphasized, in view of subsequent criticism, that although they were empirically determined, they do form a coherent pattern. The basic principle is that the language has to be represented in the form of open syllables; when two or more consonants begin a syllable they have to be shown by doubling the vowel; but when a consonant stands at the end of a syllable before a consonant at the beginning of the next, it is omitted altogether. The rules may be summarized thus:

1. Five vowels (*a, e, i, o, u*) are distinguished, but length is not noted.
2. The second component of diphthongs in -*u* is indicated (*au, eu, ou*).
3. The second component of diphthongs in -*i* (*ai, ei, oi, ui*) is generally omitted, except before another vowel, when it appears as *j*, and in the initial sign *ai*.
4. The glide which intervenes in pronunciation between an *i* and a following vowel is generally indicated by *j*, that after *u* by *w*. These sounds are ordinarily omitted by Greek alphabetic spelling.
5. There are twelve consonants:
   j (= English *y*) used only to indicate diphthongal *i* or as a glide; see 3 above.
   w = the old Greek letter digamma (ϝ), pronounced like English *w*.
   d, m, n, s with values as in later Greek (approximately as in English).
   k = *k, kh, g*; **p** = *p, ph, b*; **t** = *t, th*.
   r = *r* and *l*.
   z = Greek ζ, the exact phonetic value or values in Mycenaean times being still uncertain.
   q = a series of sounds called labio-velars (k^w, g^w, k^wh), some of which were preserved in Latin (e.g. *quis, ninguit*), but had been entirely lost from classical Greek, where according to position they appear as *k, p*, or *t* (and the corresponding stops for the voiced and aspirated forms). Their existence in prehistoric Greek had been predicted long before.
6. There is no sign for the aspirate, nor are the aspirated consonants *th, ph, kh* (Greek θ, φ, χ) distinguished from the unaspirated.
7. *l, m, n, r, s* are omitted from the spelling when final or preceding another consonant: e.g. *po-me* = *poimēn* 'shepherd', *ka-ko* = *khalkos* 'bronze', *pa-te* = *patēr* 'father'. This surprising rule can be more scientifically restated thus: the only final consonants admitted by Greek (*n, r, s*) are omitted, and this practice is then extended to medial closed syllables (i.e. before another consonant) and to other sounds of these classes (*l, m*).

8. Initial *s-* is omitted before a consonant; we also at this time extended this rule to initial *w-*, but this was later shown to be an error based largely upon wrong etymologies given by the dictionaries.
9. In groups consisting of consonant + *w* both consonants are written, the intervening vowel being either that of the following syllable or *u*; but *r* before *w* is usually omitted.
10. Stop consonants (*d, k, p, q, t*) which precede another consonant are written with the vowel of the following (rarely preceding) syllable (e.g. *ku-ru-so* = *khrusos*); similarly *mn* (as in *A-mi-ni-so* = *Amnisos*). Special measures are adopted to represent final clusters of consonants (e.g. *wa-na-ka* = *wanax*).

The syllabary was already known to contain some signs which appeared to be interchangeable, and were therefore transcribed as pa_2, a_2, etc. Further work has added to their number; but, although this method of transcription is convenient, we now know rather more of the conditions under which they were employed. For instance, pa_2 must have been in origin *qa*; ra_2 usually represents *ria*; ra_3 = *rai*, and so forth. There are also a few oddities in the system, such as a sign for *pte*, for *nwa*, and—only recently recognized—for *dwo*.

Generally speaking the spelling rules are in agreement with Cypriot, but the following differences show that the two systems were not in exact harmony. In Cypriot diphthongs in -*i* are regularly indicated; the labio-velar consonants had been eliminated from the dialect, so there is no *q*; *d* is not distinguished from *t*; but *l* and *r* are kept distinct; the use of *z* is disputed, and there seems to be a special sign for *xe*. Final consonants are shown by adding an unpronounced vowel *e*, and *all* consonant groups are treated by inserting extra vowels, except that *n* is omitted before another consonant. Much has been made of the shortcomings of Mycenaean as compared with the later Cypriot; but later products often show improvements on earlier ones, and we cannot blame the Mycenaeans if their solutions to the problems of devising a script 'are not always those which a UNESCO subcommittee might have proposed'.

'Evidence' gave a full list of the words which had provided the equations of vowels and consonants for the grid, but the undeciphered grid was suppressed—a pity, for the gradual build-up of the pattern as outlined in chapter 4 should carry a good deal of conviction. Once again we must blame the tyranny of space; no one, so far as I know, has ever complained that 'Evidence' contained too much material. However, in retrospect I can see that the section headed 'Points of Departure for an Experimental Transcription' would have been better if an attempt had been made to follow more closely the order of discovery. We did not indicate clearly enough the crucial significance of the Cretan place-names, nor did we insist that the Greek solution was imposed by these identifications; the impression was given that the names came as a check on values originally derived from identifications with Greek.

This part of the article ended with four explanations intended to disarm any critics who might protest at the incompleteness of the decipherment: (1) the dialect is 1000 years older than classical Attic, as great a gap as between *Beowulf* and Shakespeare; (2) the archives are not literary essays but highly abbreviated accounts; (3) the article represented only the first three months' work on an entirely new subject; (4) no attempt could be made to deal with all the material; attention was concentrated on the most significant tablets.

Then came a section demonstrating the variations due to gender. The best example of this was a tablet in which the masculine *do-e-ro* (classical *doulos* 'slave') was correlated with *pa-te* (*patēr* 'father') and feminine *do-e-ra* with *ma-te* (classical *mētēr* 'mother'). An analysis of the personal names showed the different types of declension, which were further confirmed by a study of occupational terms, a hundred of which were listed. Verbs are relatively rare, but four forms of the verb *ekhō* 'have' were demonstrated, and some other verbs were identified and discussed, notably the passive participles with the characteristic Greek ending *-me-no* (*-menos*). These sections provided specimens of some of the main

77

classes of tablet. One of the Knossos chariot tablets was translated thus:

> Horse-(chariots), painted crimson and with joinery work complete, supplied with reins. The rail(?) is of fig-wood, with fittings(?) of horn, and there is (no?) 'heel'(?).

Suggestions from others have since led us to improve on this version; we still do not fully understand the words translated 'with joinery work complete' and 'fittings'. The 'rail' is wrong; it should probably be some part of the bridle or headstall for the horses, and 'fig-wood' should be 'leather'. These modifications will show how far we have advanced since then; and equally how the general sense was already discovered. Most of the phrases translated will still pass muster today, though we often understand better now, after five years' work by dozens of scholars, what lies behind these formulas.

'Evidence' ended with a short section on the position of the Mycenaean dialect. We outlined the principal features of the dialect and commented on their relation to the dialects of the classical period, and to other related languages. The conclusion was already advanced, and this has not had to be modified, that the new dialect was most closely related to Arcadian and Cypriot, as had been predicted; but under the influence of the prevailing view of dialect relationship we also emphasized the links with Aeolic. Since 1952 important new work has modified the general view, and this has entailed a shift of emphasis, and the abandonment of the name proposed for this dialect, 'Old Achaean'. This has led some people to suppose that we have changed our view of the position of the dialect; actually it is a part of the background which has shifted in the meanwhile. The last words were a suggestion that the tablets would prove important for the study of Homer, a prophecy rapidly fulfilled.

Between the writing of 'Evidence' and its appearance in the autumn of 1953 we had to possess ourselves in as much patience as we could. In conversation with colleagues we had already succeeded in gaining some converts, and as a result both of us were asked to lecture on the decipherment to learned, and less learned, societies in various parts of England. In this way the ground was prepared for the article.

We had been fortunate in gaining quickly the adherence of L. R. Palmer, recently appointed to the chair of Classical Philology at Oxford, and two leading Swedish scholars, Professors A. Furumark and G. Björck of Uppsala. Their further help and support at this critical period did much to overcome the hesitations which we naturally encountered among our colleagues.

It was Furumark who gave us our first publicity, as early as November 1952, when he was interviewed by the Swedish press. He had been receiving the Work Notes, and when the Experimental Vocabulary reached him, he described it as a 'bombshell dropped through his letter-box'. The praise he lavished on Ventris caught the eye of journalists elsewhere; but too few people had then seen the decipherment, and Bennett in Yale, when asked his opinion, was studiously non-committal.

In private correspondence with Ventris, Bennett had expressed himself more freely. On 6 July he wrote: 'I don't know whether to congratulate you or offer condolences on your recent decipherment, because it came at a deucedly inconvenient time, just when I was checking entries in the index....On the face of it I don't like your freedom to supply l r m n t q w e r t, etc., but there were some other things that seemed quite reasonable.' Later that year he was still too busy to devote the time necessary to check the decipherment, and on receiving an advance draft of 'Evidence' in October wrote: 'I shall probably return now to wavering back and forth, thinking one day that you have it, and the next that you haven't.'

The lecture given by Ventris in London on 24 June 1953 was reported by *The Times*; a leading article discussed the claim and its possible consequences. The coincidence that it stood next to a comment on the conquest of Everest was not missed; and it was not long before the decipherment was being described as 'the Everest of Greek Archaeology'. But of course the one feat was certain and provable; the other was still a doubtful claim to be authenticated, and *The Times* was right to head its comment 'On the Threshold?'

We had expected that our article would touch off a long and bitter controversy before the theory was finally accepted. Scholars do not accept revolutionary changes without the deepest probing; and even then some are always reluctant. But in this we were wrong. Even before the theory could be published, Professor Blegen had put into our hands a decisive confirmation, a weapon so powerful that the failure of the opposition was certain before it had begun.

CHAPTER 6

THE DECIPHERMENT AND
THE CRITICS

One afternoon in May 1953 the telephone rang in my flat in Cambridge. Michael Ventris had called me from London in a great state of excitement—he rarely showed signs of emotion, but for him this was a dramatic moment. The cause was a letter he had received from Professor Blegen, the excavator of Pylos. We knew that Blegen had found more tablets in 1952, but no one had yet examined them carefully; they had been cleaned during the winter and only the next spring were they ready for study. Blegen's letter ran:

> Since my return to Greece I have spent much of my time working on the tablets from Pylos, getting them properly ready to be photographed. I have tried your experimental syllabary on some of them.
>
> Enclosed for your information is a copy of P641, which you may find interesting. It evidently deals with pots, some on three legs, some with four handles, some with three, and others without handles. The first word by your system seems to be *ti-ri-po-de* and it recurs twice as *ti-ri-po* (singular?). The four-handled pot is preceded by *qe-to-ro-we*, the three-handled by *ti-ri-o-we* or *ti-ri-jo-we*, the handleless pot by *a-no-we*. All this seems too good to be true. Is coincidence excluded?

The text of this now famous tablet must be quoted in full:

1 *ti-ri-po-de   ai-ke-u   ke-re-si-jo   we-ke* 〈vessel〉 2
  ti-ri-po   e-me   po-de   o-wo-we 〈vessel〉 1
  ti-ri-po   ke-re-si-jo   we-ke   a-pu   ke-ka-u-me-no   ke-re-a₂ [
2 *qe-to* 〈vessel〉 3
  di-pa   me-zo-e   qe-to-ro-we 〈vessel〉 1
  di-pa-e   me-zo-e   ti-ri-o-we-e 〈vessel〉 2
  di-pa   me-wi-jo   qe-to-ro-we 〈vessel〉 1
3 *di-pa   me-wi-jo   ti-ri-jo-we* 〈vessel〉 1
  di-pa   me-wi-jo   a-no-we 〈vessel〉 1

The interpretation of some phrases in this tablet is still disputed, but Blegen's analysis of its contents from the ideograms is evident, and the relative words are clear. Where there are pictures of tripod-cauldrons, we have the word *ti-ri-po*, that is *tripos* 'tripod' or in the dual (since early Greek has a special declensional form for two of a thing) *ti-ri-po-de = tripode* with the numeral 2. The series of vessels at the end are all called *di-pa* (or in the dual *di-pa-e*), which must be the vessel called in Homer *depas*. Two difficulties arose here: first we have the vowel *i* for Greek ε, but other cases of this have been found, and it appears to be restricted to certain words; secondly, we usually translate the Homeric word 'cup', though it is clear that in some cases it is not a drinking vessel but much larger—Nestor's *depas* was so heavy that when full a man could hardly lift it. It would seem likely that, as often, the type of vessel to which the term was applied had changed over the centuries. The first adjectives describing these vessels are *me-zo* and *me-wi-jo* 'larger' and 'smaller', two words we knew already since they are used to classify children into 'seniors' and 'juniors'. Then follow the adjectives which vary with the number of handles. The second term of the compound is always *-o-we = -ōwes* (or *-oues*) and means 'ear'. This is the word regularly used in Greek for the handles of a pot: Nestor's 'cup' had four 'ears'. The first part consists of *tri-* (as in *tripos*) for 'three', *qʷetro-* for 'four' (classical *tetra-*, but cf. Latin *quattuor*), and *an-* (the negative prefix) for no handles.

The odds against getting this astonishing agreement purely by accident are astronomical, and this was a proof of the decipherment which was undeniable. A few people have of course remained unconvinced—we will deal with their objections later on. But all who were unprejudiced could now be convinced that the system worked; further refinements would no doubt be possible, but the basis was obviously sound.

We had to admit at once that not everything on the tablet was plain sailing. For instance the three narrow-necked jars called *qe-to*; there is no Greek word which would fit that, though Bennett suggested later on that it may be an earlier form of the word we know as *pithos*. Again we are not agreed on the interpretation of the descriptions of the tripods; a number of suggestions have been made, none free from objections, and we shall probably have to wait for the discovery of more texts of the same sort before we can be sure what they mean. Then there is a point which our critics have made much of: the second entry in line 2 has the word *me-zo-e*, which is the dual form, as in the next entry, though the numeral is 1 and the preceding and following words are singular. The answer is really quite simple: the scribe has made a mistake—an easy one, if he had the next entry already running in his mind. There are quite a large number of cases where we can say for certain that the scribe has made a mistake; for instance, if a tablet has a constantly repeating formula, and in one case for no reason it is written differently, we need have no fears in putting it down as an error. After all, how many of us could write a thousand lists without letting through the occasional mistake? And once the clay was dry, it was impossible to delete the word and put it right. But of course when these mistakes occur in isolated phrases they are very hard to detect, and we have several times been led astray by errors of this sort.

The trouble with the descriptions of the tripods is not that we cannot translate them, but that we have too many possible translations and insufficient criteria to enable us to pick the right one. One phrase is clear enough to be worth mentioning: the third tripod is called *apukekaumenos skelea*, 'with its legs burnt off'. Some have taken exception to this phrase on the grounds that a useless vessel would not have been listed. It is impossible to judge this objection since we do not know the exact purpose for which this tablet was written, though it is clear that it is an inventory of some kind. Those with experience of such documents will know that not only new goods figure in them; and we have an exact parallel in some of the tablets listing unserviceable chariot wheels.

To Ventris and myself this tablet was a godsend: not that either of us wanted convincing further, but we knew that here was a proof to carry conviction with any impartial judge. Blegen did his best to hasten its publication, and Ventris was able to publish his own version in the spring of 1954 in the American journal *Archaeology*. But before that it had been mentioned in lectures, and the news had leaked out to the wide circle of scholars whose interest had been aroused by 'Evidence'.

The Hellenic Society reprinted 'Evidence' as a separate pamphlet and more than a thousand copies were sold, an event without parallel in the annals of the society. Reviews of it soon began to appear in learned journals all over the world, and not a few articles were published by newspapers and more popular magazines. How far the news of the confirmation influenced reviewers it is hard to tell; and but for that its reception might not have been so enthusiastic. A typical comment was that of Professor M. S. Ruipérez, writing in the Spanish periodical *Zephyrus* early in 1954:

Although it may be susceptible of further refinements and corrections the interpretation... (which comes to crown many years of tenacious effort by the young English architect Mr Michael Ventris) unites—let us say it at once—all the guarantees which can be demanded (reading of whole phrases with meaning suited to that expected from the ideograms, reading of known place and personal names, perfect coherence in orthography and grammar) and must in consequence be regarded as definitive.

This view was echoed by other scholars, but not entirely without criticism; indeed right from the first the decipherment was subjected to the most careful testing and probing. For example, Professor P. Chantraine of Paris, a leading expert on the Greek language, complained of the absence of a full explanation of the process of decipherment. He noted the asymmetry of the syllabary: a sign for such a rare group as *pte*, a sign for the initial diphthong *ai*, but not for the other diphthongs. The coarseness of the script too caused difficulty; it seemed too easy to make Greek words when the spelling rules allowed so much liberty. And he continued for twenty pages listing difficulties which the decipherment raised. But despite this he had no doubt that the solution was on the right lines:

> Since the decipherment of Hittite [he wrote], the discovery of Mr Michael Ventris must be considered the most important progress achieved in this field of research....His linguistic system works and obliges us to revise basically hitherto accepted ideas. The extreme difficulties of the script, the absence of real bilingual texts have as a result the fact that in detail the tablets still present many kinds of difficulty. The philology of 'Old Achaean' is still to be established. But it will advance fast, thanks to its inventor....

A more critical review still came from the very citadel of Minoan archaeology: an article written by Dr N. Platon, the director of the Iraklion Museum where all the treasures of Knossos are preserved. It was of course particularly galling to a Greek to be told by a foreigner that tablets in his own museum were written in his own language. Small wonder that he viewed the decipherment with some scepticism, and tried to find every possible hole in the argument. His verdict may be fairly summed up as 'Not proven'; but in the following years he began to change his mind.

For this I can claim a small share of credit. In the spring of 1955 I was able to spend a week in Crete working on the Knossos tablets. In the course of conversation Platon told me that since Bennett left the year before, he had found in the museum storerooms some trays containing fragments of tablets; they had been exposed to the weather when the museum was damaged during the war, and he thought they would be useless. They were certainly in a poor way; some had crumbled to dust or disintegrated at a touch. But I was able to salvage a large number of pieces that were reasonably hard. Time prevented me from making a proper job of it, and it was left for Ventris to finish later in the year. But I had one great stroke of luck. I found a largish piece which was the left-hand end of a two-line tablet; the break showed plainly half a horse's head—the ideographic sign for 'horse'. Now horses appear in the Knossos tablets only in the records of the chariot force, which have a quite different form, and in an isolated tablet showing horses and foals—a famous tablet on which Evans had identified, and discarded, the word for 'foal'. The left-hand edge of this was missing: was this the piece? I cleaned it hurriedly and carried it downstairs to the glass case where the tablet was on exhibition. I laid it on the glass; it looked a good fit. Platon came and opened the case, and the join was sure. A happy discovery; but there was something on this fragment which shook Platon's scepticism, for we now had the introductory words for each line, and they read: *i-qo* 'horses' and *o-no* 'asses'. Again Blegen's question could be asked: is coincidence excluded? What are the chances that two series of equine heads will be introduced by words exactly corresponding to the Greek for horses and asses? Such probabilities are beyond mathematical analysis; we can only have recourse to the guidance of common sense. Again difficulties have been raised by our critics: why are the asses not more markedly distinguished from the horses in the drawings? Perhaps the simple answer is that the scribe having written the appropriate words did not feel it worth the effort. It is also probable that there was a standard ideographic sign for 'horse', but none for 'ass'; what could be more natural than to employ the same sign but with the phonetic indication to show the difference?

During this period Ventris received many letters from experts abroad whom he had kept informed of his work. Their tone was extraordinarily favourable. Professor Sittig, for instance, who was committed to his own line of decipherment, was generous enough to abandon his theory and support Ventris. On 22 May 1953 he wrote: 'I repeat: your demonstrations are cryptographically the most interesting I have yet heard of, and are really fascinating. If you are right, the methods of the archaeology, ethnology, history and philology of the last fifty years are reduced *ad*

Plate II

(*a*) Horse tablet from the Northern Entrance Passage at Knossos (see p. 86).

(*b*) Tablet mentioning a shepherd from the Archive Room at Pylos (see p. 140).

absurdum.' And a week later: 'I am extremely grateful to you for your most interesting news of the new inscription, which removes all doubt and completely verifies your assumption.'

The Swedish expert on Greek and Mycenaean religion, Professor Martin Nilsson, was enthusiastic. He pointed out that if proved right Ventris' achievement would outstrip that of Champollion and Rawlinson, since they had parallel texts or at least words to start from. However, he declined to express himself definitely, as he did not consider himself competent to judge the linguistic questions. This of course was a difficulty for the archaeologists: the judgement of the decipherment was a linguistic problem. Those who knew only classical Greek were worried by unfamiliar forms; but these same discrepancies were a source of comfort to the philologists, who had already reconstructed some of them by the comparison of the classical dialects.

Professor J. Friedrich of Berlin, who had just written a book on the decipherment of unknown languages, wrote to Ventris on 12 February 1954: 'I have not yet had time to study your work thoroughly. But as far as I can see, you make a very good and well considered impression, and the individual arguments fit together so well, that you really seem to have found the right solution.' It was nearly two years, however, before he made a public profession of his adherence in a short article in the periodical *Minos*. This journal, which had been started at Salamanca as an international review of work on Minoan subjects, has now become the chief vehicle of specialized work on Linear B. At the beginning of 1956 Friedrich wrote:

Made wise by experience, I have for a long time practised reserve, if not rejection, with regard to the ingenious decipherment of the Cretan Linear B script by M. Ventris. After thorough testing of his methods and his results, however, I have now reached the firm conviction that this decipherment is in point of fact right, and has laid a sure foundation, even if, as the decipherer himself says, there is still much to correct.

The American scholar Professor I. Gelb was another who, despite surprises, was quickly convinced: 'I may tell you without further hesitation', he wrote to Ventris in November 1953, 'that I am fully convinced of the correctness of your decipherment.... The Greek discovered by you, as close to the Homeric as it is, I must confess came as a great surprise to me. Still, I do not doubt your conclusions.'

The first comments on the decipherment were mainly an exposition of the facts and a weighing of the evidence. But very soon contributions began to appear which added to our knowledge. Scholars were prepared to take our work as a foundation on which to build, and new suggestions and improvements began to come in. Furumark's long article represented a considerable advance, for he went through the various categories of tablet, and demonstrated how all could be interpreted as Greek. Palmer's inaugural lecture, called 'Achaeans and Indo-Europeans', was a stimulating and exciting account of the results of the decipherment presented with great linguistic skill. It would be idle to pretend that he and I see eye to eye in all details, and I shall have to consider his theory of Indo-European culture in the next chapter; but I welcome this opportunity of recording the great debt which Mycenaean studies owe to him.

Ventris and I were not of course standing still. We had already in December 1953 written a more popular account of the results and decipherment methods in the journal *Antiquity*. In August 1954 Ventris' lecture to the International Classical Congress at Copenhagen was a triumph; when he showed the slide of the tripod tablet deciphered the whole of the large audience burst into applause, before he had said a word. After he had finished, a number of prominent Greek scholars publicly congratulated him and declared themselves convinced. I myself was not present, and it was only gradually that I learnt from others the extent of this success; Ventris himself was too modest to tell me more than that it 'went off all right'.

The most exciting prospect now was that of reading all the new Pylos tablets found in 1952. Publication could not be hurried, but Blegen was good enough to let us see the texts in advance. Bennett, who had been finally convinced by the tripod tablet, first copied a selection of the new tablets for us, and in 1954 Ventris was able to make a complete transcript and discuss the readings with Bennett in Athens. Professor Wace also very kindly allowed us to copy the tablets found at Mycenae in 1954.

With this advantage we were strongly placed to write a full account of the tablets. Once more Ventris invited me to share the task, and our collaboration enabled us to complete a volume of 450 pages in a matter of twelve months or so. During this time we both visited Greece and checked the readings of the tablets against the originals, so that the texts we gave are not exactly the same as those edited by Bennett. Our work on the Knossos texts was published separately, with Bennett's help, in the form of a transcription into Roman script. *Documents in Mycenaean Greek* was completed in the summer of 1955, and published in the autumn of the next year, a few weeks after Ventris' death.

The book was built up of three parts; first came five introductory chapters, dealing with the decipherment, the script, the dialect, the proper names, and a summary of the resulting knowledge of Mycenaean civilization. The kernel of the book was a representative selection of three hundred tablets from all three sites, chosen to include all the most interesting and important. None were excluded on the ground that they were difficult to interpret; and many more tablets were discussed in the notes and commentary. In all but a few cases a translation was given, but with due caution, the doubtful words being indicated by italic type. Where a translation seemed impracticable the difficulties and the possibilities were fully discussed in the commentary. The last part of the book was a vocabulary containing 630 separate Mycenaean words, from all the known tablets, with their suggested meanings; and a selection of personal names which had to be restricted to the more interesting in view of the enormous number of words which could be identified as names (over 1200).

The reviews which greeted this book were generally as favourable as those which had been given to 'Evidence'. But a few weeks after the publication of *Documents* came the first serious attack. Some criticisms had already been voiced in America by Miss J. Henle, who had the misfortune to complete a statistical survey of Linear B at the same time as Ventris was publishing his theory; she was naturally hostile to a theory which differed from her own, though she too believed the language to be Greek.

The *Journal of Hellenic Studies*, which had three years earlier published 'Evidence', now gave space for a lengthy article by A. J. Beattie, Professor of Greek at Edinburgh. He had been one of my teachers at Cambridge, and as one of the leading British experts on the Greek dialects, Ventris and I had as early as 1952 shown him our tentative work, in the hope of persuading him to join us. He found himself unable to accept our arguments, and despite further correspondence he remained unmoved even in the face of new evidence which we sent him. He wrote his article without seeing *Documents*, but although this answered many of his questions, it did not succeed in convincing him, and he reviewed it in the same hostile tone in the *Cambridge Review*.

Beattie began by admitting, as hypotheses, that the language of Linear B was Greek, and that the syllabary consisted of open syllables (consonant plus vowel). He then discussed the grid, but it is clear that he did not understand how it was constructed or used, and his whole account of this stage is distorted. He tried to reconstruct for himself the initial stages of decipherment, made numerous mistakes, and ended by remarking: 'Consequently I regard the table of comparisons and the grid with strong suspicion.' The blame for not making the actual process clearer rests with us; but it is odd that Beattie, who asked us about other things, never bothered to find out what was the real order of discovery.

He admits that many words and phrases make good sense, but 'of course we do not know whether Mr Ventris used these words *in the first instance* [his italics] to establish the value of one sign or another'. This is a fair objection at first sight. Unless we are quite sure that the words cited in evidence are not the same as those put in to establish the values, the whole thing may be a delusion.

A fictitious example will serve to expose this fallacy. Let us imagine we are deciphering an English message, in which the value of the letters is unknown to us. We find in it six words, which can be classified by their position and behaviour as follows:

Nouns	XYZ	ZYX
Verbs	XY	ZY
Adjectives	XYYZ	YZZ

If we can solve one noun, the rest will come out automatically; but if we identify it wrongly, then the rest will be nonsense. In this way we can be sure that $X=G$, $Y=O$, $Z=D$ is the only possible solution.[1]

Something of this kind can be attempted with Linear B, but with a syllabary of eighty-odd signs, it is obviously much harder to find words which are merely the same syllables in different orders. But Beattie cannot reject *to-sa pa-ka-na* (Greek *tossa phasgana* 'so many swords' followed by a pictogram of a sword), because if those words were chosen to put into the grid, then *pa-?-to* emerges from it as the name of a Cretan town (*Phaistos*), *ka-sa-to* is a name (*Xanthos*), *pa-sa* is *pansan* (feminine accusative) 'all'. It does not matter what words are put in; sense will come out *only* if the values are correctly determined. Let us try this on a larger scale: here is a table in which every value occurs at least twice, and every word is plausible sense in its context:

a-ni-ja-pi	instrumental plural	*hēniai*	'reins'
a-pi-qo-ro	nominative plural	*amphipolos*	'waiting women'
a-ra-ru-ja	feminine plural participle	*araruiai*	'fitted'
a-to-po-qo	nominative plural	*artokopos*	'bakers'

[1] This anagram was first proposed by Professor L. R. Palmer, but used somewhat differently.

a-to-ro-qo	dative singular	*anthrōpos*	'man'
ka-ko	nominative singular	*khalkos*	'bronze'
ka-ru-ke	dative singular	*kērux*	'herald'
ke-ra-ja-pi	instrumental plural	*keraos*	'of horn'
ko-ru-to	genitive singular	*korus*	'helmet'
po-ni-ke-qe	dative singular	*phoinix te*	'and a phoenix'
qe-to-ro-po-pi	instrumental plural	*tetrapous*	'quadruped'

(The Greek words are given in their classical form, so are not directly comparable with the Mycenaean spellings.)

Every word identified is composed of syllables which repeat in other words, and the vocabulary of *Documents* will provide ample material for checking all but the rarest signs. It is no longer of any consequence to know how the values were obtained; the words they yield constitute their own proof. If we take into account the equations of signs which made it possible to construct the grid before decipherment, then we have a double check, because we know already that, for instance, *sa*, *pa*, *ka* and *na* share the same vowel.

To this Beattie will of course reply: not all the words make sense. For instance: *ka-na-to-po* and *ka-na-po-to* are unintelligible even if the values are right. Now if we were deciphering a message in a language we knew this would be alarming. Suppose our English cipher gave us also YXY = OGO, we should be worried, unless we discovered too that the message concerned British Somaliland, and we knew too that Ogo was the name of a region south of Berbera. Now in Linear B we have three unknowns: the subject of the tablets, except in so far as we can guess this from the ideograms; the proper names (with the exception of a few place-names); and the actual dialect of Greek in use. It is as if we were deciphering not messages in modern English, but in the language and spelling of Chaucer, *and we had never seen anything like this before*. Add to this the incompleteness of the spelling and it is obvious why we cannot interpret every word. *Ka-na-to-po* is a woman's name; *ka-na-po-to* is probably a name too, but it is on a mere fragment which gives very few clues. If we like to hunt in the dictionary we might risk *gnamptos* 'bent' for the latter; but most of us eschew this sort of gamble. We do not normally identify a word until we have some idea what sort of word it is likely to be, simply by the study of its context. But I repeat: we have no dictionary of *Mycenaean* Greek, and we have no list of *Mycenaean* proper names. All our guesses must be based on evidence many centuries later.

Palmer adduced another similar argument, which adds weight, even if not in itself conclusive. The tripod table quoted at the beginning of this chapter shows that *qe-to-ro-* is an element correlated with the numeral 'four'. It was also shown in chapter 4 how the word for 'and' was identified as the sign *-qe* tacked on to the back of the word it connects. What languages are there in which the word for 'and' has roughly the same sound as the beginning of the numeral 'four'? Greek is obviously a candidate (classical *te*, *tessares*); but others are possible, at least among the Indo-European family: for instance Sanskrit (*ca, catur*).

This brings us to a further point not considered by Beattie, but seriously raised by another critic, Professor E. Grumach of Berlin, in an article published in the *Orientalistische Literaturzeitung* for July 1957. Is Linear B Greek? Are the spelling rules merely a convenient device to enable us to equate foreign words with Greek ones? There are many ways of answering this; perhaps the simplest is to compile a list of some of the words which are accompanied by self-evident ideograms:

ti-ri-po-(*de*)	⊞	*tripous (tripode)*	'tripod cauldron'
di-pa	♉	*depas*	'vessel of some kind'
pi-a₂-ra, pi-je-ra₃	⌒	*phialē, phielai*	'dish'
a-pi-po-re-we, a-po-re-we	⌾	*amphiphoreus, amphoreus* (dual in origin *-rēwe*)	'amphora'
pa-ka-na	⚕	*phasgana*	'swords'
to-ra-ke	⚑	*thōrākes*	'corslets'
ko-ru	⚵	*korus*	'helmet'

pa-we-a, pa-we-a₂	⌷	pharea (originally *pharwea)	'cloths'
i-qo	🐎	hippos	'horse'
o-no	🐴	onos	'ass'
po-ro	🐴	pōlos	'foal'
ta-ra-nu, ta-ra-nu-we	⟝⟞	thrēnus, thrēnues	'footstool'

(Syllables which occur more than once in this list are in heavy type.)

Others less certain could be added; but the close correspondence with Greek words can be seen at a glance, and it is even closer if we substitute for the classical forms the older reconstructed ones. We must conclude that Linear B is either Greek or a language so much like Greek as to be indistinguishable from it.

Beattie and Grumach have tried to upset this list by pouring scorn on our identifications of the ideograms. It must be admitted that the helmet could be other things, and the corslet is not very clear. But the vessels are all pretty clearly vessels, the horses, asses and foals animals of equine type. And no one can deny that the tripods have three legs.

At this point it will be as well to deal with an objection which has frequently been made: that no one is likely to write the same word twice, both in the syllabic script and by means of an ideogram. This is true of scripts which are genuinely ideographic, though readers of Japanese newspapers will know that rare ideograms are regularly accompanied by the reading in syllabic signs. If, however, the ideogram is not so much a conventional sign for a word as a drawing of the object intended, it may be necessary to add a more precise definition. A picture may clearly represent a vessel, but without indicating whether it is 6 feet or 6 inches high. Its name prevents any confusion, and not only is this the regular Mycenaean practice, but the name is sometimes abbreviated to a single sign and inserted into the picture; for instance, the pictogram of a vessel at Knossos resembling broadly the Pylos *di-pa* has the sign *di* written on it. Equally the picture guarantees the correct reading of the name; verifications of this

94

kind are familiar in accountancy, witness the English habit of writing on cheques: Two Pounds, £2.

But there is another feature of Mycenaean ideograms which disposes of this objection completely. Ideograms are never used as syntactic units of a sentence: they occur only in connexion with numerals, thus: 'X and Y, MEN 2', 'footstool inlaid with ivory figures..., FOOTSTOOL 1'. For the purpose of counting it is necessary to have a unit, like the small boy who could not add 2 and 3 together, but only 2 oranges and 3 oranges. So strong was this feeling that where no ideogram existed (or the drawing would have been difficult) the scribe sometimes felt obliged to make one out of a ligature of the same syllabic signs he had just used to spell the name; 'ten cheeses' is written tu-ro_2 TU + R O$_2$ 10. In such cases the scribe would obviously not have *read* the word *turoi* 'cheeses' twice. The alleged difficulty simply does not exist.

It is hardly necessary to produce a second answer to demonstrate that Linear B is Greek. But the study of Linear B inflexion is equally convincing; I shall mention only a few striking points. There is an old Homeric genitive of nouns in -*os*: -*oio*; so Mycenaean *do-e-ro* 'slave', genitive *do-e-ro-jo*. Homer has a termination -*phi* to denote instrument or place; so Mycenaean *a-ni-ja-pi* 'with reins', *po-ni-ki-pi* 'with phoenixes', *pa-ki-ja-pi* 'at (the place) Pakianes'. Here are two examples where Mycenaean confirms the predictions of the philologists. The perfect participle active is formed with an original suffix -*wos*-, also known in other languages; but in cases other than the nominative singular this has been replaced in Greek by a new formation -*wot*-, not found outside Greek. Mycenaean shows a stage before this innovation took place: *a-ra-ru-wo-a* is the neuter plural of a participle meaning 'fitted' = classical *ararota*; Mycenaean has kept the original suffix -*wos-a*, which regularly becomes -*woa*. So too in the adjective meaning 'bigger': Attic Greek has a nominative plural masculine *meizous*, which was explained as a contraction of -*oes* (from earlier -*os-es*); Mycenaean supplies the missing link: *me-zo-e*. Other examples could be added, but they are tedious reading to those unfamiliar with the history of the Greek language.

Another argument used against the decipherment is that the ambiguities of the script would make reading impossible. That it is hard for *us*, no one will deny. But we cannot agree that an educated Mycenaean would have found the same difficulties. The objection is raised that one sign may represent as many as seventy different syllables: *ka* could be *kă, kā, gă, gā, khă, khā, kai, kal, kar, kas, kam, kan*, etc., etc. This is true; but it is not true of *all* signs: e.g. *mi* or *u* are much more restricted. But the suggestion that when you take a word of three signs, the possibilities are 70^3, is false, because some choices for one sign automatically eliminate others for the next. For instance, *s-* before another consonant is not written at the beginning of a word (as *ke-re-a₂ = skelea*); but this only gives additional options for the first sign of a word, since an *s* omitted in the middle of a word cannot be counted both as an optional beginning for one sign *and* an optional ending of the preceding one; *pa-ka-na = phas-ga-na*, so that, if *pa* stands for *phas*, this eliminates *sga* as a choice for *ka*. In any case initial *s-* cannot be omitted if the word begins in Mycenaean spelling with *j-, w-, r-, s-, z-, n-*, or probably *d-*. The choice of *kam* or *kan* is in fact illusory; it will always be conditioned by the following sign, or if final only *kan* is possible, since no Greek words end in *m*. By this means we can whittle down considerably the hundreds or thousands of readings that are theoretically possible.

But there is an even more important consideration. The reading must represent a word known to the Mycenaean vocabulary. We of course do not know the total range of possibilities; but the Mycenaean reader would have had no difficulty in eliminating all the possible readings which did not make Mycenaean words. Even so, he would sometimes have been left with a choice of two or more words, and he would have had to choose on the basis of context, just as we do when faced with written forms like *row* or *tear*. The choices of different inflexional endings must have been tiresome; but it must always be borne in mind that we have no indication that Mycenaean scribes ever attempted long and involved sentences. In the ordinary way they kept to short formulas, which must have been so familiar that there was no possibility of error. The whole question of Mycenaean literacy will be discussed in the next chapter; but we must at once protest that arguments which presuppose literacy as we know it today are invalid.

Words are recognized by literate persons as complete units, and faced with *di-pa* the reader would not have gone over in his mind all possible readings of the two signs, any more than we think of all the possible pronunciations of the groups of letters in a word like *thorough*. He would hardly need the pictogram written alongside to tell him which reading he needed. All systems of writing are only approximations to the sound of the words, and some of Beattie's arguments on this score are disingenuous. 'Pylians', he writes, '...would hardly know what to make of *pu-ro*.' There would be as much risk of a Pylian making a mistake as there would be of a Scot misreading *E'boro*.

One slight complication is purely the result of our system of transliteration. It is true that the sign transliterated *ka* can represent also *ga* or *kha*; but to the native reader the sign was not any one of these. It simply indicated a velar stop, the exact nature of which was determined by the context. It is therefore pointless to talk of a Mycenaean failure to distinguish *l* and *r*; for convenience of transliteration we have to choose one or the other (in fact we arbitrarily selected *r*), but the Mycenaeans merely used the same set of signs for both sounds. English speakers have little cause to complain, when they use *th* for two different sounds, and *gh* for a whole series. Modern languages, however, generally prefer the opposite complication: the same sound is written in many different ways.

One last point needs to be made here. When we look at our index of Mycenaean sign-groups, we shall find many words which are incomplete or occur in small fragments with no context. There is not much hope of ever finding a convincing interpretation of these. Of those that remain, the majority can be shown to be proper names; at least 65% can be proved, and the true figure is more like 75%. This can easily be demonstrated. Many tablets list single sign-groups followed by the ideogram MAN (or WOMAN) and the numeral 1. These are clearly their names, since, if they were occupational terms, they would repeat more often. Some of these sign-groups are also found in characteristic groups of tablets with standard formulas; therefore all other sign-groups which can replace these names are names too. In this way we can build up a list of names which is entirely independent of the decipherment.

But the identification of names is for us a risky business. The scribe knew the people he had to deal with; we have no legal documents in which precise naming was of vital importance. He knew well enough that *e-ko-to* spelt *Hektōr*, because there was only one man in the group in question whose name would fit that pattern. Sometimes, when there were two men whose names if not actually the same were spelt alike, he would add the man's occupation or other details to distinguish him. We unfortunately have no means of checking; once we have established from the context the fact that a word is a name, we can only guess, so it is small wonder that this side of the decipherment is much less complete and certain. We have reason to believe that a number of the names are not of Greek type, and thus we have nothing by which to identify them. But in a high proportion of cases we *can* think up a solution; often more than one, so that we cannot choose between them. But when Beattie assures us that *qe-ra-di-ri-jo* 'could not by any means be twisted into Greek', we may reply that he has not tried hard enough. The name will represent a classical *Tēlandrios*, not actually recorded, but made up of three clear Greek elements: *tēle* 'far', *andr-* 'man' and the suffix *-ios*, as if in English *Farmanson*. Other reconstructions of this name are possible, but one example is enough to refute this sort of charge.

Shortly after the publication of Beattie's article an attempt was made to start a controversy in the *Sunday Times*. An analysis of the resulting correspondence published showed that no one was prepared to advance any reasons in support of Beattie's position, whereas a great variety of arguments were put forward in favour of Ventris. If this was intended as a test of opinion, the answer was clear. Abroad Beattie's article was greeted with astonishment and derision. If he and Grumach were right, it would have meant that the foremost experts on the Greek language throughout the world had been the victims of a delusion; such matters are not to be judged by counting heads, but the authority of leading scholars in every country where Greek is studied cannot be lightly set aside.

The present state of research on the Mycenaean texts and related problems is best illustrated by some figures from the bibliographies which have been published by the London University Institute of Classical Studies. The four issues which have appeared cover articles and books from the publication of 'Evidence' down to the end of 1958. In this period alone we have recorded 432 articles, pamphlets or books by 152 authors from twenty-three different countries. This rate of work still continues, and if anything is increasing. It would be invidious to single out any particular authors, but a few comments are necessary. These figures exclude the work on the publication of the texts, which has fallen chiefly to Bennett. Two useful glossaries have been compiled in transliteration, one by Meriggi, one by Georgiev. The London Institute of Classical Studies has not only held a series of Linear B Seminars, which have provided a forum for discussion among British scholars, but has also undertaken the publication of texts and bibliographies.

The respectability of this new branch of classical studies is evident from the fact that it has been accepted as a proper subject for research degrees, and that it now appears in the examination syllabus at the Universities of Cambridge and Oxford. Needless to say, it is not yet suited for the ordinary level of undergraduate instruction, but its importance is recognized, and it will remain a growing field for specialists.

In April 1956 the French Centre National de la Recherche Scientifique, under the direction of Professors Chantraine and Lejeune, organized the first International Colloquium on the Mycenaean texts. Nine French and eleven foreign scholars from seven countries met for a week at Gif near Paris to discuss the work done and to plan for the future. Their contributions were printed in a volume entitled *Études Mycéniennes*; but the happiest result of the meeting was the friendly spirit in which we resolved our differences. Now at the first sign of a quarrel, we have only to appeal to the 'esprit de Gif', and I hope that this beginning will be followed by all who now seek to enter the circle of specialists in Mycenaean. At this meeting Ventris was of course the leading figure; his fluency in French made a great impression, but he was equally at home chatting to the Swiss in Schwyzerdeutsch, or to the Greek delegate in Greek.

Five months later he was dead; but the work he did lives, and his name will be remembered so long as the ancient Greek language and civilization are studied.

CHAPTER 7

LIFE IN MYCENAEAN GREECE

The glimpse we have suddenly been given of the account books of a long-forgotten people raises at once hopes that through this means we can now gain an insight into life in the Mycenaean age. Just as the Domesday Book is a vivid social document of life in eleventh-century England, so too the tablets cast fitful beams of light on the domestic institutions of prehistoric Greece. But there is of course a vast difference between these two sources. The Domesday Book is not an isolated document, it can be explained and interpreted by contemporary historical records. In Greece an impenetrable curtain separates the fragmentary tablets from the more complete records of the historical period; during the Dark Age which followed the eclipse of the Mycenaean civilization, the recollection of the former ways of life dimmed to vanishing point or survived, if at all, transmuted and confused in folk-memory.

Thus no apology is necessary if the picture which we attempt to give of Mycenaean life is incomplete, distorted and in many respects conjectural. Further research and discoveries will, it is to be hoped, do much to clarify the details; but we may feel confident that the outlines at least are broadly visible. All the same I feel obliged to protest against the facile guesswork which builds far-reaching hypotheses on slender evidence, and I shall risk trying my readers' patience by indicating from time to time the dangers of going too far beyond the meagre facts.

One fact stands out at once as of major consequence: the Mycenaeans were Greeks. Schliemann, when he excavated the first grave circle at Mycenae, had no doubt that he had unearthed a Greek dynasty, and in his famous telegram to the king of Greece claimed to have looked upon the face of one of the king's ancestors. But more academic judges were not so certain, and at one time theories of foreign domination were invoked to account for the precocious brilliance of the Mycenaeans at such a remove from the historical Greeks. The proof that the language of their accounts was Greek might be thought to have settled all controversy on this score; but much ingenuity has been expended on attempts to circumvent the implications of this evidence. The language of accounts is not always that of their writers: an Indian business house may find it convenient to keep its accounts in English; a medieval king of England may have had his secretaries write in Latin. But in all such cases which I know of, the language in question is a dominant literary language, and the language replaced by it a local one with restricted currency and often no adequate orthography. If Greek were adopted by foreigners as a written language, as it was in Hellenistic Egypt, then this implies that Greek was already a dominant literary language: a conclusion which on the available evidence is absurd.

Even this does not answer two theories which have been put forward: either that the preserved tablets were written by Greek scribes in Greek at the behest of foreign rulers; or that they were written by foreign scribes in Greek for Greek rulers. The best refutation of these theories is the existence in the tablets of large numbers of transparently Greek personal names, and these are not stratified but belong equally to all classes of society. For instance, a person of the highest standing at Pylos is named *E-ke-ra$_2$-wo*, which appears to be a well-known type of Greek name *Ekhelawon*; at the other end of the social scale a smith has the delightful name *Mnasiwergos* 'Mindful-of-his-work' and a goat-herd has the common name *Philaios*.

Many names of course are much harder to interpret as Greek, and some are certainly foreign; but the presence of an element foreign in origin, if not still in speech, does not contradict the positive evidence that Greeks were widely spread throughout society, and we can feel sure that the Mycenaeans were at least predominantly Greek. The 700 years or so between the coming of the Greeks and the Pylos tablets are time enough to allow the pre-Hellenic inhabitants to have been absorbed.

The presence of Greeks at Knossos is still something of an embarrassment. Professor Wace and a few other archaeologists had demonstrated the close links between Knossos and the mainland in the period preceding the fall of the Palace there, and even proposed to explain them as due to mainland influence on Crete, and not vice versa. The truth is that the limitations of archaeological research preclude deductions about the languages spoken by the people studied. The physical remains may allow an anthropological classification, but people of a given physical type do not all speak the same language. The study of 'cultures', peoples using artefacts of similar type, is the archaeologists' main weapon. It is this, for instance, which enables us to feel sure that about 1900 B.C. a wave of invaders entered and settled in Greece. But the inference that these were the ancestors of the Greeks is based upon the knowledge that Greek was subsequently spoken in that area, and could not be made without recourse to non-archaeological premises.

Thus a clear statement from the archaeologists of the date when mainland influence first appears at Knossos is a vain hope. When a half-civilized people conquer a civilized one, they try to absorb and adapt as much as they can of the superior civilization, so, especially if the actual conquest is not accompanied by great destruction, the event may easily escape the archaeologist's spade. There is, however, one piece of evidence, not strictly archaeological, which proves that the Greek domination of Crete was a comparatively recent event: the use of Linear A, apparently down to the early fifteenth century, is an indication that Greek had not then replaced Minoan as the language of accounts; unless Linear A too is Greek, a possibility which none but the most determined enthusiasts will admit.

We know not only that the Mycenaeans were Greeks, but also what sort of Greek they spoke. They were not Dorians, nor apparently Aeolians; it is tempting to follow a widespread custom and call them Achaeans, the name Homer most often uses for the Greeks as a whole. The name *Hellēnes* does not appear until after Homer, and *Greek* is of course only taken from the Roman name for the peoples of Greece. What name the Mycenaeans used—if indeed they had one at all—is still a mystery. But at least we can say that linguistically their nearest relatives in the classical period were the Arcadians and Cypriots, and next to them the Ionians.

What caused the collapse of the Mycenaean civilization is a problem which has intrigued specialists for three-quarters of a century. The decipherment leaves us no nearer a solution. There is reason to believe that the last event in this collapse was an invasion of Dorian Greeks from the wild country of the North-West; but there is still no proof that this was the principal cause. On the assumption that Pylos was expecting the attack which followed soon after the tablets were written, we can read into them references to the forthcoming event; it is obviously exciting if a series of tablets dealing with the movement of troops can be construed as preparations against an impending attack. Personally I believe this is so, but since we have no parallel documents showing the normal peacetime state of the army, we cannot be sure that these were not ordinary routine dispositions. However, if we make this assumption, the picture that emerges has several convincing details.

A number of the Pylos tablets deal with military and naval matters. A small tablet states that a contingent of thirty rowers, drawn from the coastal villages, is to go to Pleuron. There is probably at this date little distinction made between merchantmen and warships, for naval warfare was an invention of a later age. Thus a purely peaceful voyage cannot be excluded; but the danger which must already have been imminent suggests that this was no trading mission. Why were they going to Pleuron? If the Pleuron meant is the city mentioned by Homer, this is in Aetolia, on the north of the Corinthian gulf. This was certainly a Mycenaean city,

so we may hope that for once we have got a geographical identification. But unfortunately Greece, like all other countries,
duplicates its place-names; how many towns are called Newport
or Milton? So when we find a place *Ko-ri-to* we may feel confident
that this spells *Korinthos*, but what we know of the Pylian kingdom
makes it certain that it is not the famous city on the Isthmus, but
merely a small village of the same name. The same may be true of
Pleuron; though there is nothing improbable in Pylos sending a
ship to Aetolia, if that is the direction from which the attack was
coming. Despite a great deal of ingenuity it is still impossible to
determine precisely the geographical limits of the kingdom controlled by Pylos.

Two other tablets list rowers, one showing a total of well over
400, some figures being lost; the other mentions 'rowers who are
absent'. Again we are tempted to speculate: were they absent on
duty or without leave? Did the navy experience desertion in the
face of impending danger? So long as less dramatic explanations
are possible, it will be well not to build on these half-understood
phrases.

More significant are a group of tablets dealing with what they
call *o-ka*. Despite intensive study we are still not agreed on the
details, and in particular what an *o-ka* was: probably it was a kind
of military unit, perhaps a command, though some have connected it with a word meaning 'merchant-ship'; but all are agreed
that the context is military. The introductory phrase reads: 'Thus
the watchers are guarding the coastal areas.' It seems clear that the
purpose of the operation order is to establish a coastal observation
corps, and we may infer from this that an enemy landing from the
sea was feared. Ten 'commands' are listed, each belonging to a
named man; their location is sometimes given, but not always;
then follows a list of other names, presumably subordinate officers;
then the forces at their disposal, often quite small and never larger
than 110 men. All the detachments are multiples of ten, so that we
may have here a clue to the organization of the army. Each

section ends with the entry: 'and with them (is) the Follower So-and-so'. The 'Followers' (*e-qe-ta* = *heqʷetai*) are important men, presumably followers of the king and perhaps members of his household like the 'counts' of the Germanic feudal kings. Why does each unit have a royal officer, not apparently in charge, but attached? My guess is that he is the communications section. How would the watching units spread out round a long coastline make rapid contact with headquarters? Fire signals might be possible for an alarm; but a despatch rider would be essential, and the Followers, as we know from other tablets, possessed chariots—the fastest means of transport in use at that time. I think therefore that the job of the Follower was to keep the unit in touch with headquarters by means of his chariot. If this is right we begin to see a picture of the king at Pylos organizing an early warning system; he has a long coastline to defend, and he will not be able to oppose a landing at every point. But provided he has speedy news of the attack, he may be able to muster his army to meet the invaders; and fight they must, for the palace, unlike its counterpart at Mycenae, has no massive walls behind which to shelter. In the event the preparations proved vain; arrowheads and human bones found outside the palace show that it was defended; but it was burnt to the ground, never to be rebuilt.

Although the destruction of the palace was violent, we owe to that fire the survival of the clay tablets; for it can hardly be an accident that all three sites which have so far yielded tablets have been destroyed by a violent fire. Of the circumstances of the attack and the fate of the inhabitants we remain in total ignorance.

The destruction of the palace at Knossos is dated by the archaeologists some two hundred years earlier, but the similarities between the two series of records are such that many have wondered if this difference in time were not illusory. Archaeologists derive their dates chiefly from indirect methods. Careful excavation will often reveal the deposits of successive periods neatly ranged in super-imposed strata like a gigantic layer cake. The nearer the top of the cake the later the date. Examination of the surviving objects, especially pottery, enables the expert to distinguish styles typical of particular strata or periods, and the depth of these strata is also a rough indication of their length. All the dates thus obtained are relative; an absolute chronology can only be achieved by correlating strata with known historical events, if at least we except the new technique of carbon-14 dating, which does not give sufficiently accurate dates at this range to be of much help. In prehistoric periods we can only work from synchronisms with other cultures which have a recorded history, and for prehistoric Greece this means chiefly Egypt. Datable Egyptian objects were found at Knossos, and it is from these and similar finds that the date of 1400 B.C. for the destruction of the palace is obtained. Nevertheless, there remains considerable doubt about the exact date, and some slight adjustment may eventually be necessary; but it would seem impossible to bridge the gap of 200 years.

Some of the Cretan place-names played an important part in the decipherment; about a dozen are now recognizable as known classical sites. Our failure to identify the others is probably due to our incomplete knowledge of the ancient geography of the island; Homer speaks of ninety or a hundred cities on the island, but the classical number known is much less. The sites, however, which we believe we can identify with names on the tablets cover virtually the whole of Crete, and this seems to imply that Knossos exercised dominion over the whole island; on the other hand, no place-names outside Crete can be found, so it would not appear that Knossos was the centre of a maritime empire as suggested by Thucydides; that legend, if true, must belong to another era.

Military and naval organization at Knossos cannot be traced; but we do have a certain amount of information about weapons which enables us to reconstruct some facts about the army. The characteristic weapon of the period was the lightly-built two horse chariot, carrying two men; such vehicles were used for peaceful as well as military purposes, if we may judge from scenes in art.

The famous Tiryns Fresco shows two women driving in a chariot apparently on a hunting expedition. Hence we must be careful not to deduce that all the chariots on the tablets were military ones. For instance the chariot frames recorded on the Knossos tablets with ivory inlay and elaborate equipment are probably for civil or ceremonial purposes, though the royal family may have used such vehicles in the field. The wheels are inventoried separately, no doubt because they were removed when the vehicle was not in use; surprising as it may seem to us, Homer knew that the first thing to do on getting your chariot out was to

Fig. 14. A Knossos chariot tablet (Sc230).

put the wheels on: 'Swiftly Hebe put on the chariot the curved wheels, of bronze with eight spokes, about the iron axle.' Some of these details do not agree with Mycenaean evidence, though we must make allowances for the fact that Homer is describing a divine chariot. For instance, Mycenaean wheels always have four spokes, and although one pair at Knossos is described as 'of bronze' we may doubt whether the whole wheel was of this material. The usual material on the tablets is willow or elm; three of cypress-wood are recorded. Tires of some sort seem to have been frequently fitted, and some were bound with bronze; one pair was bound with silver. One Knossos tablet mentions as many as 462 pairs.

One series of Knossos tablets is undoubtedly the muster roll of the Panzertruppen or armoured brigade: each tablet records a man's name, a chariot complete with wheels, a cuirass, and a pair of horses (Fig. 14). In a few cases there is only a single horse, which may mean that the chariot was not operational. The total is not easily computed, since many of the tablets are fragments; but I count eighty-two chariot ideograms, which gives the minimum figure. We shall probably not be far wrong if we reckon on a chariot-force numbering well over a hundred. The chariot was managed by a driver (a charioteer is specifically mentioned by one Knossos tablet, but the muster-roll has only one name for each chariot, presumably the warrior); the passenger was thus free to do the fighting. In Homer chariots seem to be little more than taxicabs taking the warriors into and out of battle; but this may be, in part at least, due to the fact that Homer, writing in an age when the chariot had long been obsolete, had forgotten their true use. A formation of a hundred massed chariots charging at a gallop would have been a formidable spectacle; and it has been noticed that in one passage Homer does appear to recollect such tactics; Nestor advises such a formation, and implies that it is no longer usual. But massed chariots could only have been deployed in open country; in many parts of Greece the opportunities for such tactics must have been limited, and the chariot force would therefore have been used more as motorized infantry than as tanks.

Unfortunately the Pylos chariot inventories have not yet been found. Possibly, as at Knossos, they were kept in a separate office outside the main archive room; but they must have existed, for we have plenty of records of wheels. Here, as usual, the scribes were more explicit at Pylos than at Knossos: the wheels are carefully distinguished as serviceable or unserviceable, and some have other epithets such as 'old'. A rather surprising feature is the enumeration of wheels as 'of the Followers'. This implies that the Followers were in effect the chariotry, or at least an important part of it. Indeed the similarity of their name (*e-qe-ta*) to the word for 'horse' (cf. Latin *equus*) has made some scholars try to equate it with the Homeric word for 'knight', *hippota*. Tempting as it is, in view of all we know of Mycenaean grammar the idea must be rejected. The word for 'horse' is always *i-qo*, not *e-qo*, and all its derivatives show the *i* like the classical Greek *hippos*. The chariot

is called by a derived name: *i-qi-ja = hiqq*"*ia* 'the horse (vehicle)'.
The total number of serviceable wheels is in the region of eighty-
four pairs; but how many spares were needed for each chariot we
do not know. If the roads round Pylos were anything like what
they are today, they would not have lasted long.

The body-armour worn by the Homeric heroes has been end-
lessly debated; efforts have been made to reconcile the descriptions
with the archaeological evidence, not always with success, and we
must allow for anachronisms here as in other parts of the poems.
If we study the tablets the picture becomes a little clearer, for we
are lucky enough to have inventories of armour from both
Knossos and Pylos, and they agree in broad outline. The helmet is
of a simple conical shape; we are not told its material, but leather
is a fair guess, for it has attached to it four 'plates' or 'scales'. The
word so translated is not identified with an attested Greek word,
but the general sense seems clear from its use. How they were
arranged, or how large they were is not specified, but it may be
significant that their number is usually the same at both places,
though one Knossos tablet mentions only two. Also attached to
the helmet must have been the pair of cheek-pieces. The body
was protected by a corslet or cuirass; again the material is not
specified, but one tablet hints at linen. Attached to this were some
thirty or more 'plates' (again the same word), twenty large and
ten small, or in some cases twenty-two large and twelve small.
These figures are from Pylos, as the relative parts of the tablets are
missing at Knossos.

Here I must mention a difficulty. The corslets at Pylos are called
by their normal Greek name *thōrākes*, but this is not found at
Knossos; instead there is an object called *qe-ro*$_2$. We started by
thinking that this too meant 'corslet'; but an unpublished tablet
which was noticed at the end of 1956 made me change my mind.
There is one tablet that lists sixteen of these objects together with
some vessels, and not only tells us that they were made of bronze,
but also gives a drawing of one. It is a rough square with a curving

top, and with good will can be seen as a kind of corslet. But the new tablet was further evidence that where a single set of armour is listed there are always two *qe-ro₂*; in other words they are worn in pairs. Now a two-piece corslet made of solid metal is possible, but it is not known in Homer and is clearly not the same thing as the *thōrāx* with thirty or more plates recorded at Pylos. Moreover, the tablet goes on to mention 'shoulder-pieces' and then more 'plates', which can only be for the corslet. This persuaded me that the order was significant, and if *qe-ro₂* were enumerated between the helmet and its attachments and the shoulder-pieces they ought to be arm-guards, which would account for their use in pairs.

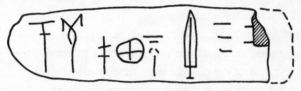

Fig. 15. A Knossos sword tablet (Ra1540).

Only at that point did I realize that there is a Greek word which fits: *pselion* 'armlet' has a variant form *spelion* which is perfectly compatible with the Mycenaean spelling.

The weapons carried by the charioteers were spears, wooden shafts tipped with bronze points ([*e*]-*ke-a ka-ka-re-a* = *enkhea khalkārea*). At Pylos bronze is requisitioned to make 'points for spears and arrows'. Swords are shown on tablets at Knossos, called by their Homeric name *phasgana*, of the broad two-edged type well known archaeologically. There is a slight difficulty here, since the type shown by the tablets is not otherwise known until a slightly later period. Pylos adds the classical word for 'sword' *xiphos*, but this would appear to be rather a thin rapier, to judge by the way it is drawn. Arrows are several times mentioned, and a labelled box of arrowheads was found at Knossos; a tablet gives two totals of 6010 and 2630 arrows.

There are two curious gaps in our picture of Mycenaean

armour. First there are no greaves, though 'well-greaved' is a favourite Homeric epithet of the Achaeans (once 'bronze-greaved'), and the archaeologists have recovered them at least from contemporary Cyprus. Secondly, and much more surprisingly, there are no shields. This is an extraordinary omission from the records; we must hope it will eventually be made good, for shields they must have had, and the figure-of-eight shield of early Mycenaean times remained a favourite decorative motif in art.

We know virtually nothing about military organization beyond what has been said above. But when we turn to the political and social structure a few details can be picked out amid the general obscurity. Both Knossos and Pylos were monarchies, for both places mention 'the king' (*wanax*) without any further qualification, which must mean that there was only one; though there is the added complication that the same title seems to be applied to gods as well. The conclusion that the kingdoms were monarchies governed by a highly organized bureaucracy could also be drawn simply from a study of the complex palaces which have been found. This fact justifies us in extending the deductions from the Knossos and Pylos tablets to Mycenae as well, where the few tablets recovered do not provide any direct evidence for the social structure.

There is also an important official called the *Lawagetas* or 'Leader of the Host', who seems to rank next to the king. I wondered at first if this might be a title for the heir apparent; but Palmer, pointing to the etymological meaning, has suggested that he is more likely a Commander-in-Chief—a view which has met with more general acceptance, though not necessarily irreconcilable with the other. What is clear is that he and the king are the only two people who have a household including tradesmen; just as we meet 'the king's fuller' so we meet 'the shepherd of the Lawagetas'. These two also share the honour of possessing a *temenos*, the name of the royal land-holding in Homer, which in later Greek has religious associations.

The same tablet which gives this information goes on to enu-
merate two other classes of land-holders, and here we encounter
a vexed question. The next class mentioned are called *te-re-ta*,
probably the classical Greek *telestai*, and there is good reason to
suppose that in some places at least they may have been important
land-holders. Palmer has built up a picture of Mycenaean society
as a feudal monarchy in which the *telestai* occupy the status of
'barons'. The Germanic parallels he adduces are at first sight
attractive and helpful. But when he goes on to postulate a feudal
system inherited by the Greeks from their Indo-European ancestors, and thus shared with Germanic and Indian cultures, it is
more difficult to follow him. This theory would imply that the
Greeks after 500 years in Greece and contact with other civilizations, especially the Minoan, had preserved their own social institutions virtually unchanged. We could believe Palmer the more
readily if in each case the titles were linguistically related; but in
fact there is the greatest diversity in the words used. Even the
Indo-European word for 'king' is shared only by Latin (*rex*),
Celtic (in Gaulish personal names like *Dumno-rix*), and Indo-
Iranian (as in Sanskrit *rājā*, whence our *rajah*); all the other
languages use different roots. And when we come to the lower
grades, Palmer is reduced to comparing words on the basis of
their *semantic* parallelism: *telestas* for instance is, according to him,
'the man of the burden', just as the Germanic *baron* may be
connected with the verb 'to bear'.

I myself have argued that the evidence will equally allow the
interpretation of *telestas* as a religious title, and this has the advantage of agreeing with classical Greek usage. But the separation of
religious and secular titles may be misleading in this context; we
have only to think of Tibet, at least until very recently, to realize
that spiritual and temporal power are sometimes hardly
distinguished.

The position of the Followers (*heqʷetai*) has been discussed
above. The Homeric kings have their companions too, but they

are called by a quite different name (*hetairoi*); so too the Germanic king had his 'counts' (Latin *comites*). The Followers wore uniform, for some textiles are earmarked for them, had a special kind of chariot wheels, and may have owned slaves in common.

The whole question of land-tenure is still hotly disputed. Despite a wealth of documents at Pylos, the exact meaning of the constantly repeated formulas remains obscure; and almost the whole of the Pylos tablets dealing with this subject relate to one village, which may not be typical. Since the majority of land-holders there have religious titles, it may be an unusual type of settlement.

The scheme of land-tenure here can be worked out in some detail, but what lies behind the bald facts is still a matter of conjecture. Land is divided into two types: *ke-ke-me-na* which is held from the community (*dēmos*) and may therefore mean something like 'common'; and *ki-ti-me-na* = *ktimenā*, which is in the hands of individuals (apparently *telestai*), and etymologically means something like 'reclaimed from the wild', 'established'; thus perhaps 'private'. The large land-holders yield a portion of their *ktimena* land to 'tenants'; but it must not be supposed that this word implies an actual lease and the payment of rent; we are still far from understanding what the economists call the circulation.

A second series of Pylos tablets relates to another village, where an annual contribution is levied for Poseidon and other mysterious entities. In this, as in all the documents, confusion arises because the land is measured in terms of seed grain, presumably the amount needed for sowing according to some fixed proportion, a method of calculation also encountered in Babylonia. Although there is an undoubted equivalence between acreage and grain quantities, it appears that some of our documents at least refer to actual seed corn rather than land.

There are a number of minor titles which are hard to define, but they have in common the fact that they do not appear in the capital itself, and are thus in some sense provincial dignities. Each village at Pylos seems to have a local official called the *ko-re-te*, perhaps a kind of 'mayor'; and he has also a deputy. The most interesting title is that of *basileus*, which in later Greek became the ordinary word for 'king'; in Homer it is still possible to see that it sometimes means a much less exalted rank; but in Mycenaean times it was clearly only a local title far below the central monarch, the *wanax*. Words do not always, as has been said, go to the bad; sometimes they come up in the social scale, as here, perhaps because during the Dark Age the great monarchies disappeared and only petty chieftains survived.

It is interesting to see that some local rulers had a 'council of elders', as if autocracy was already checked by oligarchic institutions; but we know nothing more, and cannot draw any firm conclusions from the mere existence of the word.

At the lower end of the social scale we find the slaves. How far society was founded upon slave labour we cannot tell, nor do we know if slaves possessed any rights. An elaborate index at Pylos records over 600 women, together with about the same number of children. That they are slaves is clear from a variety of indications: some are specifically called 'captives' and many are assigned to menial work (grinding corn, carrying water, spinning and so on). They are not all concentrated in the Palace, but are allocated to other places as well, possibly country houses of the royal family, since their rations are issued by the Palace. But even more interesting than their occupations are the descriptions which betray their origin. Three such epithets clearly relate to places on the eastern side of the Aegean: Lemnos, Knidos and Miletus. The last of these brings us into contact with the Hittite records, for we know that the king of Ahhijawa, who seems to have been a Greek, controlled a place on the Asiatic coast with a name like Miletus. So these places may be Mycenaean colonies or outlying possessions which traded in slaves. Alternatively, we may conjecture that they are the product of piratical raids on a hostile coast, and that the ships of Pylos ranged far across the Aegean.

Many of the tablets describe men or women by their occupations, and this enables us to form some idea of the complexity of urban life and the specialization of labour. The spinning of yarn and the weaving of cloth are women's occupations: carders, spinners and weavers are specifically named, as well as flax and wool workers. Sewing, however, appears to be done by men as well as women; we find tailors as well as seamstresses. The cleaning of garments is the task of a fuller; the king has his private fuller.

A variety of manufactures can be deduced from these occupational terms: carpenters and masons are constructional workers whom we should expect to find; ships are built by a special class of shipwrights, and caulkers are possibly a separate trade. Weapons and other metal goods are made by bronze-smiths; bronze is of course still the chief metal in use, articles of iron being very rare and never mentioned in the tablets. Lead is mentioned once at Knossos. The precious metals are gold, worked by gold-smiths, and used for some vessels and for inlay on furniture. If we look at the actual finds, we shall observe that they also made jewellery; the craftsmanship and artistry of known Mycenaean gold-work is of the highest order. Silver, which is not uncommon among the finds, occurs only once on the tablets; a fact which has made us suspect that it is sometimes mentioned under another name. The existence of bow-makers is a typical example of the degree of specialization prevailing; and the luxury trade is evidenced again by the existence of unguent-boilers, or as we should call them now perfumers. A number of tablets enable us to see a little of their work: they were issued with olive oil as the base, and this was boiled with aromatic substances to make perfumed oil and unguents. We can list three perfumes: rose, cyperus and sage. The use to which these perfumes were put is somewhat unexpected: they were sent to the shrines for religious offerings. Whether the Mycenaean ladies also used them we are not told in the tablets, but the numerous perfume flasks found in women's graves tell their own story. One mention guarantees the existence at Pylos of a physician; unfortunately we know nothing of his methods or status, except that he appears to receive a grant of land.

The existence of potters could be inferred from the well-known pottery, but it is interesting to know that one was attached to the royal household and held a fair-sized plot of land. The vessels

Knossos		Pylos		Mycenae	Transcription
200			pi-je-ra₃		BOILING PAN
201			pi-a₂-ra ti-ri-po-de	ti-ri-po-di-ko	TRIPOD CAULDRON
202	di-pa		di-pa		GOBLET?
203			qe-to	qe-to	WINE JAR?
204			qe-ra-na		EWER
205			u-te-we		JUG
206			ka-ti		HYDRIA
207	ku-ru-su-pa₃				TRIPOD AMPHORA
208					BOWL
209	a-pi-po-re-we		]-re-we	a-po-re-we	AMPHORA
210	ka-ra-re-we		ka-ra-re-we		STIRRUP JAR
211	po-ti-[ ]-we				WATER BOWL?
212	u-do-ro		u-do-ro		WATER JAR?
213	i-po-no				COOKING BOWL

Fig. 16. Mycenaean vessels and their names.

listed on the tablets, however, were probably not earthenware, which was produced in quantities too large to be separately inventoried; and in some cases they are actually stated to be of bronze or gold. But the three bath tubs recorded at Pylos were presumably of earthenware; a built-in bath, complete with a place for the sponge, was discovered in the Palace by Blegen in 1955.

We are lucky enough to have a set of records from Pylos which bear eloquent testimony to the cabinet-maker's skill. The exact purpose of the documents is disputed, but the list of items is impressive:

3 ewers	1 brush (?)
6 tripod cauldrons	2 fire-tongs
3 wine jars (?)	1 fire-rake
6 *di-pa* vessels	11 tables
3 boiling pans	5 chairs
1 ladle (?)	15 footstools
6 hammers (?)	

These items we are told were inspected on a certain occasion. Professor Palmer has suggested that this occasion was a royal interment, and that this is a list of tomb furniture; but the numbers of tables and chairs seem excessive for this purpose, and an easier translation of the disputed words makes the occasion the appointment of an official. If this official were in fact responsible for the storerooms containing precious goods, the need for an exact inventory becomes apparent; and it is easier thus to explain the note that one of the tripods is damaged. It is in this series that the famous 'tripod' tablet discussed in chapter 6 belongs. But the most interesting goods in this inventory are the furniture.

The tables and chairs are not merely listed; each piece is given a separate designation that would easily have allowed identification, and we are left in no doubt that they were superb examples of Mycenaean craftsmanship. The tables are made of marble with decorative inlays of rock-crystal, cyanus, gold and ivory. We are not sure what cyanus was, probably a kind of blue glass paste. The designs of these inlays include helmets, feather-pattern, sea-shells and spirals. The chairs were no less elaborate; here is the description of one:

One ebony chair with ivory back carved with a pair of finials (?) and with a man's figure and heifers.

Birds and lions are also mentioned as decorative motifs. Some of the footstools are matched with chairs, but the others too are just as ornate. For instance we find:

One footstool inlaid with a man and a horse and an octopus and a griffin (*or* a palm tree) in ivory.

Delicately carved plaques of ivory have long been known from Mycenaean sites—a fine collection was discovered at Mycenae itself by Professor Wace in 1952–4. It had been conjectured that these were panels inlaid in wooden furniture, which of course disintegrated in the Greek climate. Some ivories, the purpose of which was not understood, are now believed to have formed the decoration of footstools of the type mentioned. There are of course a number of problems still outstanding in such a technical catalogue as this; but there is no doubt that we have here the contemporary names for some of the motifs which have long been recognized as the favourites of Mycenaean artists.

Agricultural organization is more simple: shepherds, goatherds and cowherds show what were the principal domestic animals. In Crete a vast archive of records bears witness to the immense scale of sheep-farming, still an important industry there today. Oxen are much less numerous, and seem to have been used mainly as draught-animals; they are sometimes called 'workers'. It is fascinating to learn from the tablets what were the names given to a few yoke of oxen: Dapple, Darkie, Whitefoot, Winey, Blondie and Bawler are rough equivalents—the names of colours are notoriously inexact in the ancient languages. A reference to the class of men called 'yokers' may mean ox-drivers who attended a yoke of oxen.

Pigs were of course kept. We have a list of twenty-five which were being fattened at various villages in the kingdom of Pylos. A very few tablets mention deer; these are presumably the carcasses of wild animals. Dogs were used for hunting, if we may trust the word for 'huntsmen' (*kunagetai*), which is etymologically 'dog-leaders'. Horses are rarely mentioned except in connexion with chariots; asses are listed once.

Woodcutters are mentioned, and perhaps the 'fire-burners' we find are not just stokers, but charcoal burners; Greece was certainly much more wooded in Mycenaean times that it is today. The devastation of the forests is one of the achievements of the classical period. It is rather surprising to find that, although we have a reference to 'plough-land', no occupational terms relating to cultivation have been identified. We suggested that this might be because every household owned or rented a plot of land, and general farming was therefore not a specialized occupation; but we must be wary of negatives when so many of the terms are still not satisfactorily identified.

The staple item of food was doubtless grain, of which two kinds, probably wheat and barley, are recorded by means of ideograms. It was measured out and ground by women, but the bakers were men. This bread and porridge diet could be enlivened by spices; coriander is the most frequent, but a list from Mycenae includes also celery, cumin, cyperus, fennel, mint, pennyroyal, safflower (both flowers and seeds) and sesame. Cheese is among the offerings given to the deities, and was no doubt eaten on a large scale. Figs are another item of diet; the Pylos slave-women's rations surprisingly contain the same quantity of figs as grain. Olive oil and olives were consumed, and another ideogram is plausibly identified as wine, the existence of which can be deduced from the name of one of the oxen quoted above. The attempt of Evans and others to turn the Minoans into beer-drinkers is unnecessary, and the absence of the characteristic beer-straining vessels, as used for instance by the Philistines, argues against it. Honey occurs several times as an offering to the gods, and doubtless served as the chief sweetening agent.

An obvious question, to which there is no obvious answer, is: where did the wealth of these kingdoms come from? Articles like ivory and cumin must have been imported from the East; the copper and tin for bronze were not to be found in Greece. The only goods available for export seem to have been agricultural produce and possibly manufactured goods such as pottery, including re-exports in the form of craftsmen's work. The reconstruction of the economy is a complicated task, in which there are too many unknown factors for it to be more than conjectural. We may possibly have to take into account hidden sources of wealth in the form of loot and captives.

But we do know something of the internal economy of the kingdoms. Not only was there no coinage—coins were an invention of the seventh century B.C.—there was apparently no commodity in which values could be expressed. The other ancient civilizations of the Near East valued goods in terms of gold and silver; nothing of the kind has so far appeared on Mycenaean texts, despite numerous attempts to read such a meaning into certain texts. It was therefore necessary for the circulation of goods to be measured in kind: when villages were assessed for what we may call tribute, they were required to produce so much of a number of specified commodities. On the other hand, the central organization distributes goods to these same villages, or to groups of workers and individuals. The means by which accounts were balanced, if such a metaphor may be excused, is not known; but we can be sure that there were obligations on both sides. The difficult thing for us to grasp is the absence of anything that can properly be called payment.

Two sets of documents may be selected as typical of these operations. First, the long series of tablets from Knossos recording sheep. The totals for some districts run to several thousand, and one tablet mentions as many as 19,000. The individual entries, each on a separate tablet, follow a general plan: a man's name, apparently the owner or keeper of the flock, heads the tablet. Then we have a note of the district, and another man, who appears to be the responsible official of the Palace or tax-officer; and finally the number of sheep. Sometimes this is simply an entry such as ' 100 rams'; but more often it is broken up into categories thus: '28 rams, 22 ewes; deficit 50 rams'. This means that the total assessed was 100; the first two figures record the payment made, the last the balance due. It is significant that in these cases the total, which is not actually expressed, is almost always a round number, most often 100, but numbers like 50, 150, 200 and 300 are also found. Sundwall, who first noticed this feature, thought that the animals were oxen not sheep, and that they were hecatombs (hundreds) of sacrificial animals. The numbers involved would have made the Cretans astonishingly pious; we must be content with a less picturesque explanation. The sheep must be tribute, because a census is excluded by the round numbers and the calculated deficit. There is another queer thing about these tablets: rams heavily outnumber ewes, not merely in the deficit, which is ordinarily reckoned in rams, but in the figures of sheep received. This must mean that the keepers picked out the members of the flock least useful for its regeneration. Thus we arrive at the conclusion that these large figures represent only a fraction of the total, and a sheep population running into several hundred thousand must be supposed for the whole of Crete—by no means an improbable figure. We can only speculate on what became of the sheep thus contributed; the altar and the kitchen can hardly have accounted for them all, unless meat was eaten on a much greater scale than in classical Greece. In some cases not only sheep but wool too is recorded; the attempts to cast doubt on the interpretation of the ideogram we call wool have not, in my opinion, been successful. Here we catch a further glimpse of the mathematical ability of Mycenaean scribes, for the total of wool units is either one-quarter or one-tenth of the total of sheep, although the amounts paid and owing of each do not agree. Thus:

SHEEP	WOOL
100	$7+18=25$
50	$6+6\frac{1}{3}=12\frac{1}{3}$

or:

SHEEP	WOOL
$40+20+60=120$	$3+9=12$
$90+90\quad\ \ =180$	$11+7=18$
$80+10+70=160$	$11+5=16$

The approximation $12\frac{1}{8}$ for the exact proportion $12\frac{1}{4}$ results from the fact that the wool unit is divisible only into thirds (each of which is expressed by the weight sign roughly equivalent to 1 kilogram).

The other example is from Pylos. Here we have a series of eighteen tablets, which record the assessment of the principal villages for contributions of six commodities. Unfortunately the commodities are expressed by abbreviations and ideograms, the meaning of which we can only guess at; one is probably hides. The amounts of these commodities are calculated in the fixed proportion of $7:7:2:3:1\frac{1}{2}:150$. But fractions are eliminated, and some other small adjustments seem to be made. An ideal case is:

Me-ta-pa	28	28	8	12	6	600

Others, with the exact proportion in brackets, are:

Ri-jo	$17(17\frac{1}{2})$	$17(17\frac{1}{2})$	5	$7(7\frac{1}{2})$	$4(3\frac{3}{4})$	362(375)
A-ke-re-wa	$23(23\frac{1}{3})$	$23(23\frac{1}{3})$	$7(6\frac{2}{3})$	10	5	500
E-sa-re-wi-ja	42	42	12	18	8(9)	900
Pe-to-no	63	63	17(18)	27	$?(13\frac{1}{2})$	1350

In addition to the assessment we are given details of the actual delivery and rebates allowed, thus:

Za-ma-e-wi-ja (assessment)	28	28	8	12	5	600
delivery	20	21	5	8	6	450
remitted	1	—	—	—	—	—
owing	—	—	1	—	—	—
The *Ma-ra-ne-ni-jo* are excused the following	7	7	2	3	2	150

The deficit of 1 in the fourth column has not been recorded, nor is it shown if any credit is allowed for the overpayment of 3 in the fifth. The groups excused payment—we do not know who the *Ma-ra-ne-ni-jo* are—are most often bronze-smiths, and it is tempting to conjecture that they have a tax concession because they are engaged on vital war work, the making of weapons. For another series of documents gives in great detail the allocation of bronze to smiths at various places, and there is a reference to the fabrication of spear-blades and arrowheads.

How great was the part played by religion in everyday life we may conjecture both from the numbers of votive objects recovered by the excavators from some shrines, and from the numerous tablets which deal with offerings. Some of the earlier attempts at decipherment had interpreted a large proportion of the tablets as religious, and we were at first inclined to be sceptical of such interpretations. But from the day when I first discovered the names of three Olympian deities at Knossos, they have forced themselves upon us, and we can now find the names of most of the classical gods and goddesses in the tablets.

But it is no simple matter to identify a deity. The only ones of which we feel sure are those whose names we recognize as equivalent to classical ones. Associated with them are a host of strange names which may or may not be divine; and the presence in these lists of offerings to human representatives of the deity, such as the Knossian priestess of the winds, is a warning against jumping to conclusions.

The recognizable deities are the familiar names of classical Greece: Zeus and Hera (already coupled), Poseidon, Hermes, Athena, Artemis. *Paiawon* is an early form of *Paian*, later identified with Apollo; *Enualios* is likewise later a title of Ares; there is no way of telling whether these were, as has been held, independent deities who were only at a much later date absorbed by more prominent gods. The evidence for the name Ares is less clear. Aphrodite is so far absent from the texts, but this may be mere chance; if she really came from Cyprus we should expect the importation to have taken place in Mycenaean times, before Cyprus became cut off from the rest of the Greek world. A shock for the experts was the tantalizing fragment from Pylos with the name of Dionysos in the genitive case—and nothing else. It can be argued that it is not a divine name, but the coincidence is striking.

Homer tells us that Odysseus stopped 'at Amnisos, where is the cave of Eileithyia'. With this clue the archaeologists were able to locate a cave on the coast of Crete, not far from Knossos, which had been in use as a shrine from Minoan times onward. What then was more natural than to find a tablet at Knossos recording the despatch of a jar of honey to Eleuthia at Amnisos? Eleuthia is a known form of the name Eileithyia, the goddess of child-birth.

At this point we begin to pass from the known to the unknown: the Knossos dedications 'to all the gods' are not really intelligible, for such a pantheistic cult was not known before Hellenistic times. The worship of the winds is another unfamiliar cult, though it is not unknown. But the most curious divine title is a well-known Greek word: Potnia, the Mistress, or as we should say, Our Lady. Once this title is coupled with Athena in a way that recalls Homer's use of the word as a title for any goddess; but as a rule the word stands alone or in connexion with a place-name: 'Our Lady of the Labyrinth' is surely the most striking dedication to come out of Knossos. The usual view in modern times is that the classical Greek religion is to some extent a coalescence of two distinct beliefs: a group of Olympian or celestial deities, a concept shared by other Indo-European peoples; and a chthonic or earthly group, living in the underworld, and dominated by a goddess of fertility known to the classical Greeks as Demeter. We know from Minoan and Mycenaean monuments that a female deity played a prominent part in their religion, and I have therefore suggested identifying Potnia with this figure. No certainty is to be reached in such matters, and we must be careful not to equate Potnia with the classical Demeter. It is true that some have thought that the name Demeter is to be found in a text from Pylos; but it is plain from the context that the goddess herself cannot be meant, and we can only understand her name as used by a figure of speech for corn-land; but other interpretations are possible. There is, however, a powerful argument in favour of a mother-goddess to be drawn from a tablet discovered at Pylos in 1955, which records an offering of oil to the 'Divine Mother', a title strongly reminiscent of the later 'Mother of the Gods'. It can hardly be denied now that a cult of this type was known in Mycenaean Pylos.

A host of minor deities are probably to be recognized in the tablets. Zeus and Poseidon both appear to have female counterparts: Diwia and Posidaeia. Iphimedeia, who is in Homer a mysterious semi-divine figure, also receives divine honours. A figure whose name appears to mean the 'thrice-hero' is enigmatic. Erinys, a Fury, may be mentioned at Knossos. But beyond this we tread a realm of conjecture in which there is nothing to guide us.

The gods are mentioned in one capacity only, as the recipients of offerings. These are sometimes animals, and we can presume a ritual of sacrifice. Poseidon on one tablet receives: 1 bull, 4 rams, quantities of wheat, wine and honey, 20 cheeses, some unguent, and 2 sheep-skins. This sounds like the provision for a ceremonial banquet, and an interesting illustration of such a ceremony is to be found on a painted sarcophagus from the Cretan site of Hagia Triada. But the commonest offerings are of olive oil. A series from Knossos are lists of quantities sent to miscellaneous divinities; but a parallel group was lacking from Pylos until 1955, when Blegen uncovered the oil magazines at the back of the Palace. In these were found large storage jars and a group of tablets recording the distribution of the oil, most of which was perfumed as described above. The recipients are usually Potnia, Poseidon and the king, who in this context may be a god, perhaps only another name for Poseidon. In two cases the oil is described as 'for a spreading of couches', a name for a ritual meal offered to the images of the gods well known both in later Greek and in Roman rites; the Latin name, *lectisternium*, is strangely reminiscent of the Mycenaean term *lekhestrōtērion*. In another case we are told that the perfume was 'for the anointing of robes'.

One of the oddest omissions from our list of Mycenaean occupations is that of scribe; here the omission is almost certain to be due to our ignorance of the correct word, and the title may underlie one of the many uninterpreted words of this group. We might have expected the classical Greek word *grapheus* to be in use, for *graphō* 'write' meant originally 'scratch', a suitable designation of the process of writing on clay. But the Cypriots of classical times preferred another word, *alinō*, meaning originally 'paint'; and if, as in so many things, the conservative Cypriots had retained an old word for 'write' we might expect this root in Mycenaean. We do once meet some men called *aloiphoi*, but they may be painters or even greasers rather than scribes.

Akkadian cuneiform tablets frequently bear the name of the scribe who wrote them; but not a single Mycenaean tablet has a signature of this kind. It would appear that the writing of a tablet was not a matter of pride to the scribe; we have no parallel to the scribe of Ugarit who signs himself 'master-scribe'. Nor apparently was there any need to have the responsible scribe's name as a check against wrong entries. However, modern ingenuity has to some extent triumphed over this tiresome omission of the ancients. Bennett has made a thorough study of Mycenaean handwriting, and although the full results are not yet published, it is already clear that a large number of hands are represented at each site. Each scribe has his own idiosyncrasies; and to the practised eye the Linear B script shows just as much difference as modern handwriting. Few tablets are in 'copper-plate'; many are carelessly written, and there is plenty of scope for variation when the script uses so many characters.

The tablets found in one building at Mycenae produced evidence of six different hands; and the complete collections of Pylos and Knossos each required thirty to forty scribes to write them. These figures would be without significance, were it not certain that all the tablets from each site are contemporary within narrow limits. How can we tell that tablets 50 years old were not in the archive room when it was burnt? The answer, as so often, is indirect. If you are keeping accounts for a period of years, you must date them in a way which will enable you to know which belong to the current year and which to past years. But, again unlike many Akkadian texts, Mycenaean tablets never have a year date. Hardly any have a date at all; those that have (and they seem generally to be religious texts) are dated by the name of the month alone. Six month-names are known at Knossos, two at Pylos; and there is no overlapping between the sets as known so far; one of the Knossos month-names recurs in classical Arcadia.

By contrast there are several mentions in the tablets of 'this year' (*tōto wetos*), 'next year' (*hateron wetos*), and 'last year's' (*perusinwos*). These phrases would be meaningless, unless the tablets were current only for a year. This seems to imply that at the beginning of every year the clay tablets were scrapped and a new series started.

But, someone will say, the dates may have been not on the documents themselves, but on the filing cabinets. There is an answer to this too. We know a good deal about the filing system from the excavators' reports. Some tablets were apparently kept in wooden or gypsum boxes; but the majority seem to have been stored in wicker baskets, and when complete the 'file' was marked by a clay label. We have a fair number of these, distinguishable because their back is marked by the pattern of the basketry, where the soft clay was pressed into it. They are in general rather badly preserved, and it was only recently that I thought of trying to sort them according to the tablets they had labelled. A few were obvious; and others could be restored by comparison with the relative tablets; but in no case did the label appear to have borne more than a few words serving to classify the contents. For instance, the basket containing the corslet tablets was baldly labelled 'corslets'; one of those dealing with wheels was more explicit; it read 'serviceable wheels for Followers'. It is clear that these labels did not contain the missing date.

Another argument also confirms the absence of old records: the absence of duplicate sets. Every year similar sets of returns must

have been compiled; yet with two possible exceptions no duplicate sets have been discovered. Neither of the exceptions is a
simple duplicate; one gives additional details, the other appears
to be a writing up, with minor changes, of the information on one
set of tablets into a tabulated form. Thus the records of previous
years are clearly absent from our finds; and this means that all the
tablets from each site can be safely presumed to have been written
within twelve months or very little more. By such a roundabout
means we reach the conclusion that writing was by no means a
rare accomplishment in the royal palaces.

But how many people outside could read and write? First, we
must set aside an argument that looked promising at one time.
This was tne suggestion that the tablets from Mycenae were found
in private houses; I regret having to differ from Professor Wace
who dug these buildings, but although they are outside the walls
of the citadel, there is no reason why they should not have been
appendages of the Palace. Wace called them the houses of mer-
chants; but it is open to question whether all trade at this period
was not in the hands of Palace officials, and some internal evidence
in the tablets may point that way. It appears then dangerous to
cite the six hands in one house as proof that private households
could read and write.

There is, too, a negative piece of evidence which cannot be
dismissed on the ground that insufficient sites have been excavated.
There is not a single stone-cut inscription known in Linear B; no
grave-stone bears the name of the dead, no public building the
name of the builder. But for the tablets and inscribed jars, we
should still think of Mycenaean Greece as illiterate. And this is
the more remarkable because Linear A inscriptions have been
found on stone and metal objects in Crete.

Clearly literacy was not universal; but before we conclude that
it was the privilege of a small class of scribes, we must consider yet
another piece of evidence: the inscribed jars. These have been
found at four sites other than those where tablets occur, and at one

at least, Thebes, the jars are fairly certainly of local make, not imports. Therefore writing was not restricted to the three cities with archives. Moreover, there is little point in painting an inscription on a jar before firing it, unless it is intended that someone should read it. It would be easier to judge the purpose of these inscriptions if we could interpret them more certainly. As far as we can see at present the inscriptions are chiefly personal names: possibly the maker, perhaps the user. They are not dedications— there is nothing to suggest that the Mycenaeans thought of their gods as able to read—nor do they seem to refer to the contents. Summing up, we may conclude that writing was fairly widely practised as a tool of administration, but that it had not made much headway outside bureaucratic circles; the highest as well as the lowest members of the community may have been illiterate. The close connexion of writing with Palace administration will explain its failure to survive the upheavals which destroyed the strong centralized governments.

The character of the script, with its fine lines and delicate curves, in striking contrast to the contemporary Cypro–Minoan script (see p. 20), is also an indication that clay was not the only material used for writing; the signs are much more suited to writing with pen and ink. If so, papyrus was already in use in Egypt; a serviceable paper was made out of strips of this reed stuck together with Nile water. Alternatively, some kind of skins may have been prepared for the purpose; Herodotus in fact tells us that 'the Ionians' once used skins as writing material. Clay then will perhaps have been the second-class material used only for rough work and temporary records, designed to be scrapped once the records had been transferred to permanent ledgers. This seems natural enough to us, for we cannot imagine a civil service unable to refer back to records of past years; but we ought perhaps to pause before supposing in a Mycenaean clerk or official the same interest in the events of yesteryear. He may well have seen no point in keeping last year's accounts once they were closed.

It may also seem odd that such a useful invention as writing should be confined to such humdrum uses. Why should not letters, histories or even poems have been written down? The clumsiness of the script imposes a limitation; we may question how far a document in Linear B would be readily intelligible to someone who had no knowledge of the circumstances of its writing. It is rather like shorthand; the man who wrote it will have little difficulty in reading it back. But a total stranger might well be puzzled, unless he knew what the contents were likely to be. Thus the existence of books and a reading public is unlikely from the outset. The chances that the archaeologist's spade will one day reveal a Mycenaean library are slender indeed. But what of letters? Here the case is rather different, for if we may judge from contemporary letters in other languages, a letter at this date was still in form, if not in practice, an instruction to the messenger. At Ugarit, for instance, the regular formula at the beginning of a letter is like this: 'To the king, my master, say...' or 'Thus the king of the country of Bîrûtu to the Prefect of the country of Ugarit, my son, say...'. Linear B would be equal to this mnemonic function.

It may be not irrelevant to mention that Ventris and I succeeded occasionally in sending each other messages written in Linear B in an imitation of the Mycenaean dialect. One such was sent to mark the completion of the manuscript of *Documents*. It read in translation: 'John to Michael greetings. Today I handed over the book to the printers. Good luck! Cambridge, June 7.' Ventris commented that it was considerably easier to read than most tablets.

Lastly, we must deal briefly with a thorny problem: what light do the tablets cast on the Homeric poems? It is a difficult question, because its answer depends upon many factors outside the scope of this book; to treat it fairly would demand a full description of the world Homer depicts, a detailed review of the archaeological evidence for Greek life between the fifteenth and seventh centuries

B.C., a discussion of the process of composition of the poems and their transmission down to the present day. At present there are two schools of thought: those who believe that the Mycenaean element in Homer is great, and those who think it is small. A compromise is here possibly the best solution. We cannot deny that many features of the Homeric world go back to Mycenaean originals. To take a famous instance, Homer describes a curious kind of helmet made of felt to which are sewn rows of plates cut from boars' tusks. This was an unexplained oddity until a tomb was opened which contained a great number of pieces of boar's tusk, and Wace demonstrated that they could be mounted so as to make a helmet just such as Homer describes. But a helmet of this type can hardly have been known in the eighth century B.C.; its description must have been handed down for centuries—and if one detail, why not others? Again, the queer archaic language which Homer uses; it must have sounded to the classical Athenians rather like Spenser's *Faerie Queene* to us. Elements in it clearly come from a Mycenaean source: the case-ending *-phi*, for example, is unknown in any later dialect, but is common in Mycenaean. All this can be made to add up to a strong case for the preservation of a large Mycenaean element in the epics; to this school of thought the Trojan War is a historical event, and Homer a guide book to Mycenaean Greece.

On the other hand, where we can compare the evidence of the tablets with Homer in any detail, discrepancies are immediately obvious. The position of the king may well be the same in both Homer and the tablets; but what has happened to his second in command, the Lawagetas? Not only is his name unknown to epic verse (it could not be made to fit the scansion), but there is no term which serves instead. So, too, repeatedly with other features; it is all very well to say that Homer is not interested in the details of land-tenure, but even the common Mycenaean term for a plot of land never occurs in the poems. Several Pylos tablets list in a consistent order a group of nine important villages; the coincidence that Homer, in the Catalogue of Ships, also assigns nine towns to the Pylian kingdom was quickly noted. But the two lists do not match; Homer's includes Pylos, that of the tablets excludes it; and only one of the remaining eight names is the same in both lists. The language contains Mycenaean elements, it is true, but much is of far later date, and the old and new are mixed in such confusion that the frantic attempts of scholars to separate them have produced little agreement or real progress. It would seem best neither to exaggerate nor to underestimate the Mycenaean relics in Homer.

Whatever position is finally adopted in this controversy, it is fair to say that the decipherment has brought an entirely new element into the Homeric problem. It has provided the dumb monuments of prehistoric Greece with a linguistic commentary, incomplete and obscure, but a guarantee that their makers were Greeks. It has pushed back some seven centuries the date of the earliest Greek inscriptions, and thus extended our knowledge of the Greek language, which now has a continuous recorded history totalling thirty-three centuries, a record rivalled only by Chinese.

CHAPTER 8

PROSPECTS

The Linear B script is deciphered; what remains? What is the task that Michael Ventris has left to us, his friends and colleagues? There is a great deal still to do, and with the methods he taught us we have high hopes of further, if less spectacular, successes.

The decipherment has already triggered off a fresh series of attacks on the other two unknown scripts of the Aegean world: Linear A, the Cretan script, and Cypro-Minoan, the Bronze Age script of Cyprus. Linear A is obviously a close relative of Linear B, if not its immediate ancestor, so it would appear a reasonable working hypothesis to assume that the values of the signs which are closely similar in the two systems should be approximately the same. This provides a starting-point; but the application of phonetic values does not immediately yield recognizable words. It would be a great stroke of luck if the language proved to be akin to one already known; but failing this, it will be necessary to proceed by the steps laid down by Miss Kober and followed by Ventris: the texts must be analysed, the meanings of words or formulas deduced, the structure of the language worked out, and eventually a grid prepared by which to check the values transferred from Linear B. The first steps on this road have already been taken, and a number of scholars in different countries are devoting their time to this problem; but we are forced to admit that further progress seems for the moment to be barred by the inadequacy of the material available. Some more tablets in Linear A have been found but not yet published; we must hope that these and further finds will increase the volume of inscriptions to the point where a verifiable decipherment becomes possible. In the meantime there is of course a temptation to take the short cut of assuming identity or kinship with a known language, and extracting sense by suitable adjustments of the phonetic values. A recent claim by the American expert on Semitic languages, Dr C. Gordon, to have identified Linear A terms with words used in Babylonian Akkadian seems to be premature; others too have speculated on Semitic affinities, and it is not impossible that the solution will be found along these lines. Others, however, have favoured the idea that Linear A contains an Indo-European language, possibly related to Hittite and the other early languages of Anatolia.

The Cypro-Minoan tablets, described briefly in chapter 2, are also still too few for rapid progress. Here we have the added handicap that the repertory of signs is not yet fully known, and it is impossible to equate certainly the different signaries. This is rather like reading several different varieties of handwriting; with a knowledge of the alphabet and the language in use, it is fairly easy to read even unfamiliar scripts; but here, where we know neither script nor language, we are still floundering in uncertainties. It will take a lot more work and a lot more texts to resolve this initial problem. Moreover, the resemblance between Linear B and Cypro-Minoan is much less marked than between Linear B and Linear A, so that it is much harder to guess the phonetic values. On the other hand, we have a second clue in the Cypriot syllabary of classical times, though here too the resemblances are difficult to follow out and may prove treacherous. There is, however, the great hope that further large finds of material will be forthcoming, since all the evidence indicates that clay was the normal writing material in Cyprus, and the main archives are yet to be found. We must hope that political troubles will not interfere with the prosecution of the excavations, both in Cyprus and on the Syrian coast, from which we expect so much.

Linear B itself still remains obscure in many details. There are a number of signs which are still not certainly identified; further work may help us to clear these up, but we cannot make much progress unless we find more examples of these rare signs. A recent brilliant piece of detection will, however, illustrate the sort of discoveries still waiting to be made. It had been noted that the word transliterated *wo-wo* in certain contexts appeared to mean 'two', though it did not correspond to the appropriate Greek word; there was also a case where a name *wi-du-wo-i-jo* was apparently misspelled *wi-wo-wo-i-jo*. Professor E. Risch of Zürich then observed that in both these cases the signs for *wo-wo* were abnormal: the second was reversed, so as to be the mirror image of the first, which had the normal form. He therefore deduced that this group should be read as a compound sign with the value *du-wo* (better perhaps *dwo*), which gives us the correct Greek word for 'two' (*duō*) and explains the spelling of the name.

Rather similar is the position of the ideograms: we have had some successes, as for instance when the meaning OIL was suggested for an ideogram, and this was afterwards confirmed by a new text which associated the Greek word for 'oil' with it. A number of the less common ideograms are still unknown or very doubtful. The relationships between the various symbols for weights and measures are now fairly well worked out; but there still remains the problem of their absolute values. Ventris made some comparisons and calculations which established rough limits for these; but it remains to verify his work and improve on it. One way in which it may be done is this: large numbers of storage jars for liquids have been found by the archaeologists; now it is likely that their capacities bear some relation to the standard units of liquid measure—just as a collection of milk-bottles today would show consistently the values $\frac{1}{2}$, 1 and 2 pints. We must not expect such consistency in hand-made vessels, but there is a good chance that if enough specimens can be measured a rough average will emerge.

The most important direction of progress undoubtedly lies in the interpretation of texts that we can already translate. In the first stages of the decipherment we were thrilled to find translatable words which gave plausible sense; now we are asking what were the facts that gave rise to these records. Careful study, not of individual tablets, but of complete series is beginning to yield a general picture of the Mycenaean economy, as I tried to show in the last chapter. We have, too, to compare the results with similar documents which have been found at a number of sites in the Near East; for no civilization exists entirely in isolation, but is influenced by the traditions and customs of the other peoples with which it comes into contact. No doubt some of our present ideas are imperfect; but there is every reason to expect that the continued labours of a great variety of scholars will bring about advances in our knowledge of the real background, of which the tablets are merely one product.

But it is idle to pretend that there are not limits to the gains which can be won by continued re-examination and reappraisal of the material we possess. Some small progress may be registered when the numerous fragments of tablets at Knossos have been thoroughly examined to see if they will allow us to complete more imperfect tablets. But our chief hope must be the discovery of new texts.

That this is no vain hope has been shown by the history of the last few years. There are undoubtedly more tablets to be found. The excavation of the buildings at Mycenae where Wace found tablets in 1952 and 1954 is not yet complete; and further sites in the same area may now seem attractive to the archaeologists. The latest news of the discovery of a further eighty tablets at Pylos shows that this site is not yet completely exhausted. None the less we must now be approaching the end of this source. The British School at Athens is exploring some of the outlying buildings of the Palace of Knossos in the hope of finding, among other things, more tablets.

There are also more Mycenaean sites which may repay excavation. An important palace has recently been discovered at Iolkos in Thessaly, which it is tempting to identify with that of Peleus the father of Achilles. It is not impossible that clay tablets were in use here too, though it lies outside the main Mycenaean area. Unfortunately a modern village overlies the site and full excavation will not be possible. The same situation is blocking by far the most promising site known, that of Thebes, where inscribed jars were found during some hurried excavations preliminary to rebuilding. Thebes was one of the most important cities of Greece during the early part of the Mycenaean period; but it declined in about 1300 B.C., an interesting fact that agrees with the legend of its defeat by the army of Adrastus from Argos.

Other sites are waiting to be found. Sparta, for instance, was the seat of a Mycenaean kingdom, that of Menelaus, the husband of Helen; but his palace remains unknown. The mentions of Pleuron in the Pylos tablets suggest that this site might be worth investigating, for the location is already known. It must be remembered, however, that the discovery of a Mycenaean site is no guarantee of the recovery of tablets; two of the most famous sites, the Palaces of Mycenae and Tiryns, yielded nothing. Only where a disastrous fire happened to bake the clay tablets is there much hope of recovering records.

These are no simple or easy tasks. The experts who can conduct such excavations are few, and there are many other demands on their time. Above all, work of this kind is expensive, and it is expense that produces no direct return. By a wise decree all archaeological finds are the property of the Greek state, and they go to swell the impressive collections of Greek museums. This is as it should be, for it is far more satisfactory to have all the material relating to a culture assembled in one place than scattered over the face of the globe. Fortunately both the foreign Schools of Archaeology in Greece and the Greek Archaeological Service are awake to the need for more knowledge of the Mycenaean period. Let us hope they will be supported generously enough to make possible fresh discoveries.

If this seems an odd and obscure way of advancing the sum of human knowledge, it is worth reminding ourselves that European civilization is founded upon three great traditions: the Hebrew, the Greek and the Roman. Of these, it is in the Greek tradition that all European art, in the widest sense, has its roots, and it remains true that all that has been achieved by European artists, writers and thinkers has been profoundly influenced by the extraordinary successes of a small people of antiquity. Our debt to the Greeks is sufficient reason for wanting to know more of the beginnings of their civilization, long before the historical period.

One more great name must now be added to the list of British philhellenes who are honoured by the scholarly world, that of Michael Ventris. For us who are proud to continue his work, his simplicity, brilliance, modesty and wit will be an inspiration. Many kind things were said of him after his death, but to me none was so simple and touching as the verdict of Professor Dumézil: 'Devant les siècles son œuvre est faite.'

POSTSCRIPT

MAY 1992

For the second edition of this book in 1967 I wrote a short Postscript bringing the story of the decipherment up to date. Now twenty-four years later I have another chance to revise what I wrote then. I shall only attempt to mention a few of the more important developments since the early days of the decipherment.

At the time this book was first published, several attacks on the decipherment had already appeared, and others followed. The critics were in due course answered by the supporters of the decipherment, and this debate had the good effect of clearing up some of the obscurities in the history of the decipherment. For instance, it was suggested that Ventris did not learn of the 'tripod' tablet as described above (p. 81), but had already based the decipherment on the words it contains. This calumny was easily refuted by Professor Blegen, for the fragments making up this tablet only came out of the ground in the very weeks when Ventris was writing Work Note 20, and were then unreadable until they had been treated and cleaned; so that even if Ventris had been present at the dig, he could not have obtained the text. The astounding suggestion was then made that Ventris had earlier, by some unspecified means, obtained another tablet with similar contents, which he used and then destroyed; such speculations have done nothing but discredit the authors.

Naturally enough, those scholars who had previously committed themselves to the view that Linear B could not contain Greek have been reluctant to admit their error. Other critics have started from preconceived notions about the nature of the writing. 'That the Greek of the time', wrote one[1], 'by a kind of

---

[1] W. Eilers, *Forschungen und Fortschritte*, 31 (1957), pp. 326–32.

shorthand left out the endings and wrote so to speak only the stem of the word is the most inconceivable of all possibilities.' Looked at from the point of view of our modern alphabets it may well seem strange that the Greeks of the Mycenaean Age were content with so ill-adapted a system. But we must remember, and the evidence goes on increasing, that the Mycenaeans never used Linear B except for accounts, inventories and similar brief notes; there is no example of continuous prose, which would demand a system providing an accurate notation of inflexional elements; the script is appropriate to its actual use, which is no more than an elaborate kind of mnemonic device. We must therefore not criticize the Mycenaeans for having failed to devise a system of writing as efficient as that of their oriental neighbours.

The debate over the correctness of the Ventris decipherment has now been definitively resolved. This does not mean that there are not still a few unbelievers, but Greek scholars in every country where the language is studied have now come to accept the decipherment as valid. A few critics have tried to dispute some of the values, apparently not realizing that they stand or fall together; it is impossible to make piecemeal changes in the system. There are of course many problems still awaiting solution, but progress has been remarkable, thanks to the co-operation of many scholars in many countries.

Mycenaean is now a recognized branch of the Greek language, the subject of University courses and examinations. The results of the decipherment are used by all who seek to understand the Bronze Age in the Aegean, the seed from which the later achievements of the classical Greeks grew. I have written elsewhere about the picture of Mycenaean Greece which has emerged from work on the documents in my *The Mycenaean World* (Cambridge, 1976). I shall concentrate here on matters concerning the script.

★

Postscript

A considerable amount of new material has come to light, both from new sites and from those previously known, though nothing yet to rival the great archives of Knossos and Pylos. A few small fragments have been recovered from outlying areas at Knossos, but the most astonishing discovery has been the vast numbers of small fragments found by Evans, but never recorded or judged worthy of publication. It has become clear that Evans did not treat his finds with the precision and care which we have come to expect of a modern excavator; with a large force of workmen and only one professional assistant it is hard to see how he could have done so. He himself recorded the story of how one of his workmen, named Aristides (a name famed in antiquity as a model of probity), stole a batch of tablets and sold them in Athens; the man was convicted on the evidence of Evans's notebooks, but some of the tablets were never recovered, and those that were remained in Athens for 60 years before they were restored to Crete.

But it has become clear that Evans made no attempt to record every fragment. Influenced perhaps by excavators in Assyria who recorded only large and well-preserved tablets, he allowed thousands of small or damaged pieces to be stored away and forgotten. Some of these were found by Bennett in Iraklion Museum in 1950; more were shown to me in 1955 (p. 85).

As late as 1984 further batches of fragments were found in the storerooms of Iraklion Museum and have now been added to the collection. Most of the fragments are in themselves of little interest; but they are all pieces of tablets, and if we can find where they belong they are often helpful in completing a damaged text or supplying a new word. The task of re-uniting the tablets has been enthusiastically undertaken by an international team. To give some idea of the complexity of this task it can be regarded as trying to do three thousand small jigsaw puzzles simultaneously, knowing that many of the pieces are irretrievably lost. We make no claim to have found all the possible joins; but where we have enlarged or completed texts, this has obviously made their interpretation easier. I must pay tribute to my colleagues, Dr J. T. Killen (Cambridge), Dr J.-P. Olivier (Brussels) and Professor L. Godart (Naples); with their help and that of others a new *Corpus of Mycenaean Inscriptions from Knossos* has been edited and is in course of being printed.

The Pylos archive received much better treatment from its finders, who made their discoveries public as soon as practicable. Professor Blegen continued his work on the site up to 1964, and considerable numbers of tablets coming from the various outlying buildings were added to those previously known from the Archive Room. Fortunately some of the new discoveries were missing pieces from important tablets. One completed a broken tablet of the furniture series (see pp. 117–18). We can now add to the list of items two portable hearths or braziers. But it is typical of the present state of our knowledge that for every addition which yields immediate sense we have another that poses a problem. This same fragment gives us three new words which we have not yet succeeded in solving; but we need not despair of a solution, as our knowledge of the dialect and the material culture grows.

A number of the new tablets come from a region at the back and side of the living quarters of the palace which was probably occupied by the royal workshops. As at Knossos, many of the craftsmen must have plied their trade under the eye of the king and his officers. There is an interesting series of requisitions of labour from the provincial towns; a total of 118 men is recorded on the surviving tablets, but in each case some of the men are said to be missing.

A further group is clearly the records of the saddlers' shop. I now think that the men called literally 'sewing-men' should not be translated 'tailors' (as on p. 116), but rather 'leather-workers, saddlers'. There is an elaborate list of harness of various types and other equipment for horses such as halters and head-stalls.

Next we hear of deer-skins, which lend added point to the fragmentary records of deer mentioned on p. 119. Finally a large tablet, now almost complete, lists ox-hides and skins of sheep, goats, pigs and deer, and some of the objects made from them, such as thongs, sandals and laces.

In several cases the new texts have enabled us to correct earlier opinions. For instance, as evidence of the presence of Greeks in the ruling class I referred to the name *E-ke-ra₂-wo* (p. 102) as transparently Greek. A new tablet seems to present a variant spelling, which taken together with a better understanding of the value of the sign *ra₂* (as *rya*), suggests that our interpretation was mistaken. It is still possible to explain it as a Greek name, but it must be removed from the category of names with obvious Greek meanings. Instead we may substitute *A-pi-me-de*, which is the Greek name Amphimedes; he is a person of importance at Pylos and his name recurs at Knossos. Another important indication in the same sense is the purely Greek title of the second gentleman in the land, the *Lawagetas* or 'Leader of the Host' (p. 112).

Another interesting advance in our knowledge concerns the Mycenaean name for the chariot, which at Knossos is called simply *hiqquia* 'the horse (vehicle)' (p. 110). The Pylos tablets recording chariots have still not been found, but a new text describing wheels shows that the word *wo-ka* is probably *wokha* 'vehicle'; it is in fact from the same root as the English word. Previously, although mentioning this as a possibility, we had favoured another interpretation, and had been severely criticized by Palmer. for doing so. It is a pleasure to acknowledge yet another of his valuable contributions. The reason for our mistake is typical: the word *wokha* is an addition to the Greek vocabulary; Homer knows only the cognate plural form *(w)ok-hea*. Again there would be no difficulty in reading the tablets if we only knew the language of the time; instead we have to learn of the existence of new linguistic forms by a process of deduction, and only a variation in the formula allowed us to be sure of the interpretation.

The first Linear B tablet from Mycenae itself was found in 1950, but in 1952–4 Professor A. J. B. Wace excavated a series of houses just outside the Citadel walls, which yielded some interesting documents, especially a set dealing with spices such as coriander and cumin. Among the tablets found in this dig is a large tablet, almost complete, which consists of personal names, some of which had already been recorded at Mycenae. It would appear to be a list of twenty-four women, most of them entered in pairs. In two cases the second half of the entry consists of the words 'and daughter' in place of another personal name. Two of the new names are not merely well-known Greek names, they are names which have remained popular, in various forms, in Europe down to the present day. They are: *A-re-ka-sa-da-ra* or Alexandra and *Te-o-do-ra* or Theodora. Yet again we ask Blegen's question: is coincidence excluded? What are the chances that a random combination of six signs will yield so exactly a common Greek name?

Subsequently work by another British archaeologist, Lord William Taylour, on a house inside the walls produced some more badly preserved tablets. Their presence is a proof that the Palace must have had a major archive; but if it was in the buildings at the top of the hill, it was probably lost through denudation. Even so, we cannot help wondering whether some would not have been found, if the earliest excavators, Schliemann and Tsoundas, had known what to expect.

Less than ten miles from Mycenae lies the great fortress of Tiryns, probably built to protect the main harbour of the area, though the sea has now receded from it. This was thoroughly excavated by Schliemann and others in the pioneering days, and here too they found no tablets. But more recent work by the Germans on the town lying beneath the Cyclopean walls has produced a number of pieces of Linear B tablets. The most interesting thing about them is that they belong to many different types, which suggests that they are the scattered remnants of a major archive rather than the specialized records of an outlying store.

I referred to Thebes (p. 138) as 'by far the most promising site known' for finding more tablets. This was partly because jars with painted Linear B inscriptions were already known from earlier excavations there. But my remark that they were 'fairly certainly of local make' must now be corrected. A new technique has been developed of analysing samples of clay to determine the impurities in the material; as with the 'finger-printing' methods now used on DNA, the analysis often allows the origin of an earthenware jar to be determined. The inscribed jars from the mainland, which are found chiefly at Thebes, have now been shown to come from western Crete. This was not wholly unexpected, because some of the words on them are place names also found on the Knossos tablets. They perhaps carried a manufacturer's name and their place of origin.

In 1964 and again in 1970 small batches of tablets were found at different places in the central section of the modern town, and it is therefore very probable that a major palace, with its archive still intact, lies under the modern buildings. When rebuilding takes place, the archaeologists have a chance to dig; but the depths at which the Mycenaean levels lie make this a difficult operation. The most recent find, from yet another site in the central area, is of a series of sealings, small lumps of clay with a few words written on, accompanied by and sometimes over the impression of a seal. One of the most interesting discoveries has been the Mycenaean form of the name of Thebes itself (*te-qa*) and of two towns which are on the offshore island of Euboea.

Lastly, in 1989–90 four small fragments of tablets have been found at Khania, the principal town today, as in antiquity, of western Crete. The ancient name is *Kudōnia*, and this is found on the Knossos tablets. We have now direct proof of a Greek state in Crete apparently later than the destruction of Knossos, though this will revive the continuing argument about the date of the Knossos tables (see p. 152).

Needless to say much progress has been made in extending and refining our understanding of the script. Not all the signs have yet been given a value, because some are exceedingly rare, or appear only in a few proper names. No. 16 in the table at the front of the book can now be firmly identified as *qa* (rather than *pa₂*), but this is not very important because the syllable k^wa developed in later Greek to *pa*, so it helps with etymology rather than interpretation. Nos. 34 and 35 have been shown by new discoveries to be variant forms of the same sign, but its value still remains obscure. The existence of signs with the values *nwa* (No. 48) and *dwe* (No. 71) suggested there might be others of this type. We can now add two more, *twe* (No. 91) and *dwo* (No. 90). This last was previously thought to be a doubled *wo* (No. 42), and in fact may have been so in origin. *Dwo* is a variant form of the numeral 'two' (usually *duo*), and in one place it was added to the figure 2 to guarantee the correct reading, like our use of both words and figures on a cheque. I have proposed the values *swa* and *swi* for Nos. 82 and 63 respectively, but so far these remain unconfirmed. Among the vowel signs we now have No. 85 = *au*; No. 25 = *a₂* has been accepted as standing for *ha*, even where it occurs in the middle of a word; but aspirates are often simply omitted by the script.

Similarly progress has been made in identifying the ideograms which are not mere pictures. Ideally we can equate the sign with a Greek work spelled syllabically, but sometimes the equation is more complicated, as the following example demonstrates.

We had identified a sign used with liquid measure as meaning 'wine'; it is not dissimilar to the Egyptian hieroglyph, since both signs probably started as a picture of a vine growing on a frame.

The value was confirmed by its discovery on a sealing from the wine-store at Pylos. But on one tablet the sign also appears as if cut in half by a vertical line, and we had tentatively suggested that this indicated 'new wine' or 'must'. Olivier working in Iraklion Museum was cleaning a Knossos tablet listing wine; many tablets as found had incrustations of lime. He was surprised to find that one sign had a word written over it in tiny characters. When he reported the reading to me as *de-re-u-ko* my first thought was that *de* might be a misreading of the similar sign *ke*, because the Greek word for 'must' is *gleukos*, which in Linear B would be spelled *ke-re-u-ko*. Olivier replied to my query confirming the reading; but by this time I had thought of another possibility. *Gleukos* was akin to the adjective *glukus* 'sweet', a root which survives in English in such words as *glycol* or *glycerine*, so it presumably meant in origin 'sweetness'. But *glukus* had no obvious cognates in other languages, though it had been suggested that it might have a common origin with Latin *dulcis*, if we postulated a change of *dl-* to *gl-* for Greek. Now if the alleged change took place after the Mycenaean period, this meant that 'must' in Mycenaean would have been *dleukos*, and this answered exactly to the Linear B spelling.

A more straightforward example is the discovery by Olivier on a Knossos sealing of a picture of a long rectangular object. It turned out to be a bath, because it was accompanied by the word *a-sa-mi-to* which must be the Homeric word for a bath-tub, *asaminthos*.

Much more significant is the way in which the tablets are now being treated not as isolated linguistic specimens, but as parts of larger files which contained records of the economy of the country. The work of interpretation here is hampered by the incompleteness of our surviving archives; but many tablets which in isolation appear obscure or uninformative yield interesting information when seen in their proper context. What we have tried to do, whenever possible, is to reconstitute the files—baskets or boxes—in which the tablets were originally stored. Then by comparing a whole series of tablets we can often learn a great deal of the facts the Mycenaean clerks were anxious to record. For them the important part of a tablet was the numerals; the rest of the text was only a heading to indicate to what the numerals referred.

This allocation of tablets to their original files has been very much aided by the study of Mycenaean handwriting. All our documents are hand-written, and each scribe has his own ways of forming signs, which allows us to establish which tablets were written by the same scribe. It also enables us to estimate the number of scribes at work in the Palace. The results are surprising; there seem to be at least forty hands represented at Pylos, and no less than seventy at Knossos. This means that writing was not a specialized skill restricted to a small professional class, but we must presume that every official could and on occasion did write documents, though some hands clearly belong to secretaries who worked in many groups of tablets. This throws an interesting light on the bureaucratic organization of the Palaces.

A brilliant piece of work on these lines was undertaken by Dr J. T. Killen at Cambridge. He made a careful study of all the Knossos tablets, more than 800 of them, which refer to sheep and wool. We had thought that these indicated payment of tribute to the Palace; but it is now clear that they record the actual flocks, composed mainly of wethers, which were kept for their wool. Other flocks were primarily for breeding purposes. A search for parallel records disclosed that in medieval England records of flocks were kept that showed striking likenesses to the Mycenaean tablets, and it was thus safe to infer that the principles of flock-management were similar, and so too was the profit. For it is clear that the wool was woven into cloth, and its export must have provided much of the wealth which is

Postscript

evident in the luxury of the Palace, just as medieval England throve on trade in wool and woollen goods. This is a new historical fact that could not have been learnt by purely archaeological means.

A similar analysis of the Pylos tablets leads to the conclusion that wool, though important, was not the mainstay of the economy. Flax and linen, hardly mentioned at Knossos, were here apparently more important; and the large number of bronze-smiths—a total of around 400 is indicated—suggests that the export of metalware may have been a feature of the Pylian economy. Luxury trades are evidenced at Mycenae by a new series of texts which refers to *cyanus*-workers, the makers of the blue glass paste so much admired by the Mycenaeans for inlay work.

The method I suggested (p. 136) for determining the absolute values of the units of the Mycenaean system of measure has been applied by Professor Mabel Lang[1] to all the jars from Pylos which are sufficiently intact or restorable. It seems that for the capacity of the smaller vessels there is no noticeable grouping; but among the larger vessels peaks in the graph occur around 2.4 and 3.2 litres. The difficulty is to know which Mycenaean units the figures are likely to present. A factor of 0.8 litres can be explained in several ways. Ventris and I proposed in *Documents* a rough equation as follows (the single capital letters are the new system of transcribing the sign):

$$
\begin{array}{lclcr}
\triangledown & = & Z & & = & 0.5 \; l. \\
\triangleright & = & V & (= Z\,4) & = & 2 \; l. \\
\mathsf{T} & = & T & (= V\,6) & = & 12 \; l. \\
\end{array}
$$

This could be adjusted to agree with Miss Lang's findings either, as she suggested, by a drastic reduction of Z to 0.2 l., so that 2.4 and 3.2 l. will represent V 3 and V 4; or by a smaller

[1] *American Journal of Archaeology* 68 (1964), pp. 99–105.

adjustment of Z to 0.4 l., so that 2.4 and 3.2 l. will represent V 1 Z 2 (=V 1½) and V 2.

The choice between these alternatives is not simple. It depends upon the rations issued to parties of men, women and children; and there is not yet any general agreement on more than a few of the basic figures. Thus we know that the ration for women manual workers is T 2 of wheat per month (either 4.8 or 9.6 l.). Professor Palmer has argued strongly for a figure close to Miss Lang's, but 0.16 l. of wheat per day sounds to me a very low figure, and for a variety of reasons I think the higher alternative is the more likely. If so, the figures given in litres in the Appendix (pp. 158–61) and elsewhere in the book should be reduced by 20 per cent.

One of the most hotly disputed arguments has raged around the date of the Knossos tablets. There is of course nothing in the tablets themselves by which they could be dated; all we can say is that in content, format and script, but not so much in language, the Knossos tablets show some differences as compared with those from the mainland. These are consistent with, but do not prove, the view that they were written a century or more earlier. A small group of Knossos tablets may perhaps belong to a different period, but there is little doubt that the bulk of the archive is strictly contemporary.

The argument must be settled on the archaeological evidence; and where this is ambiguous, we cannot now check it by re-excavating the Palace. Evans destroyed the evidence by his own dig and subsequent reconstruction. Following up suggestions by others, Professor L. R. Palmer unearthed Evans' excavation note-books and re-interpreted them as proving that the tablets belong to the thirteenth century. Expert archaeologists, however, sprang to Evans' defence, and the general conclusion is that his date of 1400 may need to be lowered to around 1375, but not to the next century. Further digging of other buildings at Knossos has revealed scraps of tablets, but none in a securely dated context. Nor does the new discovery of tablets at Khania, where the date is fairly certainly thirteenth century, prove anything about Knossos. It is not impossible that Mycenaean power in Crete moved to the west of the island after the great destruction at Knossos.

We still do not know how the Mycenaeans of the mainland were able to seize control of central and western Crete, but the archaeological evidence points strongly to a date of about 1450 BC as the likely time for this event. The Minoan centres other than Knossos show signs of destruction around this date, and tombs begin to be found containing weapons, which earlier are absent. This would be consistent with a Mycenaean occupation, bringing the Greek language for the first time to Crete. But we still cannot explain why the brilliant and flourishing Minoan civilization collapsed so suddenly.

The late Professor S. Marinatos of Athens had long ago suggested that the cause lay in the violent explosion of the volcanic island of Thera, which lies about sixty-five miles north of Iraklion. All that survives today is a crescent-shaped island with another smaller island which continues the circle; these are the remains of the vast caldera produced when the central cone blew up in a gigantic eruption. The only similar event in historical times was the eruption of Krakatoa in Indonesia in 1883.

Thera had been colonized by the Minoans, and Professor Marinatos excavated part of a large town on the south coast of the island, where buildings several stories high have been preserved by being filled with volcanic ash. The archaeological date of its abandonment is the end of Middle Minoan IA, generally thought to equate with an absolute date of around 1500 BC. But the geologists have tried to date the eruption independently and have proposed a date in the later seventeenth-century, well over a century earlier than the archaeological date.

This dispute is still unresolved. But whichever is correct, it is hard to see how the cataclysm on Thera can have produced devastating results on Crete fifty, not to say two hundred, years later.

It is just possible that the cloud of volcanic ash carried over Crete devastated agricultural production; it is conceivable that the tidal wave or *tsunami* would have swamped harbours along the north coast of Crete and destroyed the shipping there. Neither of these events seem likely to have so sapped Minoan power and will to resist that the Greeks would have easily overcome them, for they seem to have had plenty of time to recover before the Greek invasion. Future discoveries will probably elucidate this problem, but for the moment the picture is becoming not clearer, but more puzzling.

The end of the Palace of Knossos is equally shrouded in mystery. There is nothing in the tablets which hints at any impending disaster. Unlike Pylos, there is no sign of military preparations; the economy appears to have been functioning normally up to the moment when the Palace went up in flames. We can speculate about an uprising by the indigenous inhabitants against their Greek masters; but all we can say is that the mixture of Greek and non-Greek names implies that the races were becoming integrated. If the earlier date is right, Greek control in the subsequent period may have been restricted to the western end of the island. If the later date is right, then Knossos will have suffered the same fate as the major Mycenaean centres of the mainland.

The successful decipherment of Linear B has naturally led to numerous attempts to apply the same methods to Linear A. There has been a welcome increase in the number of Linear A texts known, and these have been meticulously collected and published in a Corpus by L. Godart and J.-P. Olivier. We have been able to interpret the Linear A tablets as economic documents roughly similar to some of the Linear B ones. The same ideograms were in use and the numerals are easy to read; only the system of recording fractions is different, and the details of this are still not elucidated. The total number of tablets in Linear A, however, still remains far too small for the direct application of Ventris' methods.

More inscriptions have been discovered on portable objects, and the repeating formulas strongly suggest parallels with the dedicatory inscriptions common in classical Greece. But all attempts at identifying the language have so far failed. We can, however, give an approximate phonetic value to most of the Linear A signs on the assumption that Linear B assigned the same values to them; there are good reasons for thinking this assumption is correct. Thus the meaning of one Linear A word is certain; the signs which in Linear B would read *ku-ro* are used to introduce totals in much the same way as *to-so* and *to-sa* in Linear B (see pp. 46, 65). If we could find a language which used a word like this for 'total' or 'so many' we might have solved the problem. But although many solutions have been proposed, none has so far proved acceptable.

For the identification of the language group to which 'Minoan' might belong there are three obvious possibilities. It might be an Indo-European language, that is to say, allied to Greek, though the attempts that have been made to decipher it as Greek of any type have all failed. There was in use in Anatolia in the Bronze Age a group of languages belonging to a branch of this family, of which Hittite is the best known. Linear A is fairly certainly not Hittite, but a case was made by Professor Palmer for taking it to be a related language, similar to the Luvian which was spoken at the time in the south-west of Anatolia. There is a word which recurs frequently in the dedicatory inscriptions with the spelling *a-sa-sa-ra* with different suffixes. This might be, but does not have to be, the name of a deity, and Palmer ingeniously interpreted it as the Luvian form of a word which in Hittite means 'mistress'. If so, it would be a close parallel to the Greek goddess *Potnia* of Linear B (see p. 125). Unfortunately it has not proved possible to confirm this suggestion by other words, and we must await clearer proof.

The second possibility is that the language belongs to the large Semitic family, which includes Hebrew, Assyrian and the language of Ugarit. Here too promising signs appeared, such as a root *k-l* meaning 'all'. Professor Cyrus Gordon of Brandeis University, Massachusetts, suggested a great many more identifications, but it has become clear that it cannot be any Semitic language known to date.

As one who is not committed to any theory, I feel that, although one of these or the many other researchers on this subject may have stumbled on a clue, it is at present quite impossible to judge which, if any, is right. It seems to me at least equally probable that Minoan is a language which died out without trace and has no known cognates. If so, we shall only succeed in reading the texts when we have enough of them and ones clear enough in structure to enable us to deduce the meanings of the words by their contexts.

The Phaistos Disk (see p. 19) has continued to attract enthusiastic amateurs, but it is still uncertain whether this is a formalized variant of the hieroglyphic script of Crete, or an import from elsewhere. The statement that the direction of writing is from right to left has been frequently attacked; but there is no doubt that the signs were stamped in this order, and the onus of proof is on those who assert that the maker started his inscription at the end and worked backwards. It has also been demonstrated that the total number of signs in the script is greater than the 45 actually used; statistical techniques indicate around 55 as a probable size for the signary and even higher figures are not excluded. Thus the inference that this too is a simple syllabic script is confirmed.

*

Lastly, it is a pleasure to record the international co-operation which was initiated by our French colleagues at Paris in 1956 and has continued to grow ever since. We have held a series of Colloquia at places as scattered as Pavia (Italy), Wisconsin (U.S.A.), Cambridge (England), Salamanca (Spain), Neuchâtel (Switzerland), Nuremberg (Germany), Ohrid (Yugoslavia) and Athens (Greece). Large Congresses have had sections devoted to Mycenaean Studies, and in 1967 the first International Congress solely on this subject took place in Rome. The Centre of Mycenaean and Aegeo-Anatolian Studies founded in Rome on the initiative of Professor C. Gallavotti has continued to promote the subject and to subsidise relevant books. A Permanent International Committee for Mycenaean Studies has been set up and is affiliated through the International Federation for Classical Studies with U.N.E.S.C.O. It has been a great privilege to be able to spend my career contributing to the development of this new branch of scholarship pioneered by Michael Ventris.

MYCENAEAN TABLETS IN
TRANSCRIPTION

A number of tablets have been quoted or translated in the course of this book; here are a few more samples which will illustrate the nature of these documents. The text is given in Roman transcription of the Linear B; ideograms are represented by English words in small capitals, thus MAN. The details of the interpretation will be found in *Documents in Mycenaean Greek*, the reference to which will be found after the number of the tablet; PY = Pylos, KN = Knossos.

Following the text is an attempted reconstruction of the actual sound of the words used, as a Mycenaean scribe would have read them. Much in this is of course conjectural, and these transcripts are intended rather to enable those with some knowledge of Greek to see how we extract the meaning from the text. The Greek is written in the Roman alphabet, owing to the difficulty of representing certain of the sounds in the Greek alphabet. It is impossible to give a satisfactory rendering in classical Greek which is not a translation, since some words have different meanings and many have different forms.

The translation given here differs slightly from that printed in *Documents*, chiefly in suppressing indications of doubt. It must be stressed that in many cases alternative renderings are possible.

1. PY Ae134 (Plate II (*b*); *Documents*, no. 31)

> *ke-ro-wo po-me ,a-si-ja-ti-ja o-pi ta-ra-ma-⟨ta⟩-o qe-to-ro-po-pi o-ro-me-no* MAN I
>
> *Kerowos*(?) *poimēn Asiatiāi opi Thalamātāo qᵘetropopphi oromenos* ANER I
>
> Kerowos the shepherd at (the place) Asiatia watching over the cattle of (the man) Thalamatas.

Mycenaean Tablets in Transcription

2. PY Ad676 (Documents, no. 10)

pu-ro re-wo-to-ro-ko-wo ko-wo MEN 22 *ko-wo* 11
Puloi: lewotrokhowōn korwoi ANDRES 22 *korwoi* 11

At Pylos: twenty-two sons of the bath-attendants, eleven boys.

3. PY Eb297 (Documents, no. 140)

i-je-re-ja e-ke-qe e-u-ke-to-qe e-to-ni-jo e-ke-e te-o
ko-to-no-o-ko-de ko-to-na-o ke-ke-me-na-o o-na-ta e-ke-e

WHEAT 3 T 9 𝌆 3

hiereia ekhei qᵘe eukhetoi qᵘe etōnion ekheen theon
ktoinookhoi de ktoināōn kekeimenāōn onāta ekheen

PUROS 3 T 9 𝌆 3

The priestess holds (this) and claims that the deity holds the free-hold (?), but the plot-owners (claim) that she holds (only) the leases of communal plots: 474 litres of wheat.

4. PY Er312 (Documents, no. 152)

wa-na-ka-te-ro te-me-no
to-so-jo pe-ma WHEAT 30
ra-wa-ke-si-jo te-me-no WHEAT 10
te-re-ta-o to-so pe-ma WHEAT 30
to-so-de te-re-ta MEN 3
wo-ro-ki-jo-ne-jo e-re-mo
to-so-jo pe-ma WHEAT 6
Wanakteron temenos
tossoio sperma PUROS 30
Lāwāgesion temenos PUROS 10
telestāōn tosson sperma PUROS 30
tossoide telestai ANDRES 3
Worgiōneios erēmos tossoio sperma PUROS 6

The estate of the King, seed at so much: 3600 litres of wheat. The estate of the *Lawagetas*: 1200 litres of wheat. (The lands) of the *telestai*, so much seed: 3600 litres of wheat; so many telestai: 3 men. The deserted (?) (land) of the cult-association: seed at so much: 720 litres of wheat.

5. KN Gg702 (Documents, no. 205)

pa-si-te-o-i me-ri AMPHORA 1
da-pu₂-ri-to-jo po-ti-ni-ja me-ri AMPHORA 1

pansi theoi'i meli AMPHIPHOREUS I
Daburinthoio Potniāi meli AMPHIPHOREUS I

To all the gods, one amphora of honey.
To the Mistress of the Labyrinth (?), one amphora of honey.

6. PY Fr1184 (*Documents*, page 217)

ko-ka-ro a-pe-do-ke e-ra₃-wo to-so
e-u-me-de-i OIL 18
pa-ro i-pe-se-wa ka-ra-re-we 38
Kōkalos apedōke elaiwon tosson
Eumēdeī ELAIWON 18
paro Ipsewāi klārēwes 38

Kokalos repaid the following quantity of olive oil to Eumedes: 648 litres of oil.

From Ipsewas, thirty-eight stirrup-jars (?).

7. PY Ta722 (*Documents*, no. 246)

ta-ra-nu a-ja-me-no e-re-pa-te-jo a-to-ro-qo i-qo-qe po-ru-po-
de-qe po-ni-ke-qe FOOTSTOOL I
ta-ra-nu a-ja-me-no e-re-pa-te-jo ka-ra-a-pi re-wo-te-jo so-we-
no-qe FOOTSTOOL I
ta-ra-nu a-ja-me-no e-re-pa-te-ja-pi ka-ru-pi FOOTSTOOL I
(twice)

thrānus aiaimenos elephanteiōi anthrōqᵘōi hiqqᵘōi qᵘe polupodei
qᵘe phoinikei qᵘe THRANUS I
thrānus aiaimenos elephanteiois karaāphi lewonteiois s- - -nois
qᵘe THRANUS I
thrānus aiaimenos elephanteiāphi karuphi THRANUS I

One footstool inlaid with a man and a horse and an octopus and a griffin (or a palm tree) in ivory.
One footstool inlaid with ivory lions' heads and grooves (?).
One footstool inlaid with ivory nuts (?).

8. KN Sd0401 (*Documents*, no. 266)

i-qi-jo a-ja-me-no e-re-pa-te-jo a-ra-ro-mo-te-me-no po-ni-[ki-jo]
a-ra-ru-ja a-ni-ja-pi wi-ri-ni-jo o-po-qo ke-ra-ja-pi o-pi-i-ja-pi
WHEEL-LESS CHARIOTS 2
hiqqᵘiō aiaimenō elephantei ararmotmenō phoinikiō
araruiai hāniāphi wriniōi opōqᵘōi keraiāphi opiiāphi HIQQUIO 2

Two chariots inlaid with ivory, (fully) assembled, painted crimson, equipped with reins, with leather cheek-straps (?) (and) horn bits (?).

9. PY Sa794 (*Documents*, no. 291)

ka-ko de-de-me-no no-pe-re-e WHEEL ZE 1
khalkōi dedemenō nōphelee HARMOTE *ze(ugos)* 1

One pair of wheels, bound with bronze, unfit for service.

INDEX

Achaeans, 104
acrophonic principle, 28
agriculture, 119–20
alphabet, Greek, 8, 158
Amnisos, 63–4, 66, 125
Arcadia, 10
Arcadian dialect, 12, 78, 104
armour, 110–11
arrows, 111, 124
Artemis, 124
Asine, 30
Athena, 124–5

Basque, 27–8
bath, 149
Beattie, A. J., 90–2, 94, 97–9
Bennett, E. L., Jr., 15, 19, 37–9,
    44–5, 47, 50, 52, 79, 89, 99, 127,
    143
Björck, G., 73, 79
Blegen, C. W., 36–7, 80–2, 84, 89,
    117, 126, 141, 144, 146
Bossert, H. T., 47

chairs, 118
Chantraine, P., 84–5, 100
chariots, 78, 106–10, 145
cheese, 95, 120, 126
children, words for, 34, 46, 50, 64–5
Chinese language, 42, 133
Clarendon Press, 17–19
coriander, 64, 120
Corinth, 105
corslets, 110–11, 128
Cowley, A. E., 34, 46
Crete, 1, 7, 8, 10, 24, 38, 103, 107,
    119, 122, 153
cryptography, 41, 48, 67
cuneiform, 21, 27, 32, 127
Cypriot
    dialect, 78, 104, 127
    script, 17, 22–3, 27, 30, 32, 43, 49,
    76
Cyprus, 12, 20, 124, 135

dates recorded on tablets, 128
Davis, S., 155
deer, 119, 145
Demeter, 125
determinatives, 32–3, 52

Dionysos, 124
Documents in Mycenaean Greek, ix, x,
    49, 89, 90, 92, 131, 158
dogs, 119
Domesday Book, 101
Dorians, 10, 103–4
Dumézil, G., 139

economics, 7, 120–1, 137
Egypt, 12, 107
Egyptian, 27, 41
Eileithyia, 125
Eilers, W., 141
Enkomi, 20
Etruscan, 26–7, 34, 40, 48, 50
Evans, A. J., 1, 7–8, 12, 15–20, 26,
    29, 32–4, 38, 44–5, 86, 120, 143,
    152
'Evidence for Greek Dialect in the
    Mycenaean Archives', 72–9, 84

figs, 120
Followers (heq^{u}etai), 106, 109, 113,
    128
footstools, 95, 118–19, 160
Friedrich, J., 87
Furumark, A., 79, 88

Gelb, I., 88
Georgiev, V., 27, 31–2, 48, 99
Gif, Colloque de, 100
Godart, L., 144, 154
gods, 70, 124–6, 159–60
Gordon, C., 135, 156
Gordon, F. G., 28–9
grain, 114, 120, 126
Greek language, 9, 22, 48, 60, 62,
    64–5, 68, 70, 94–5, 133
grid, syllabic, 50, 57–61, 69, 74, 90,
    134
Grumach, E., 47, 93, 94, 99

Hagia Triada, 13, 126
helmets, 92, 110, 132
Henle, J., 90
heq^{u}etai see Followers
Hera, 124
Hermes, 124
Herodotus, 130
Hittite, 27–8, 31, 48, 115

162

Index

Homer, 6, 8, 78, 104, 107, 109–12, 115, 125, 131–3
honey, 120, 126, 160
horses, 33, 86, 108–9, 119
Hrozný, B., 27–8, 33, 48

ideograms, 42, 44–5, 94–5, 136
Iolkos, 137
Iraklion (Herakleion, Candia), 19, 85
ivory, 108, 118–20, 160–1

Japanese, 43, 94
Jars, inscribed, 30, 129–30

Khania, 147, 153
Killen, J. T., 144, 150
king, 112–13, 115, 126, 132, 159
Knidos, 115
Knossos, 8, 13–16, 18, 25, 62, 73, 103, 106–7, 112, 137, 143, 152–3
Kober, A. E., 19, 35, 45, 48, 54, 62, 134
Ktistopoulos, K. D., 30, 48, 51

labyrinth, 9, 125, 151
land-tenure, 114, 132, 159
Lang, M., 143, 151
language, Greek, *see* Greek language
Lawagetas, 112, 132, 145
Lejeune, M., 100
Lemnos, 115
Levin, S., 141
Linear A, 154–6
linen, 152
literacy, 127–31
London University Institute of Classical Studies, x, 99

manufactures, 116–19
Marinatos, Sp., 153
measures, *see* weights and measures
Melos, 13
Meriggi, P., 99
metals, 116, 120
Mid-Century Report, 47–9
Miletus, 115 ·
military organization 104–12
Minoan civilization, 9, 15, 18, 24, 36, 113
Minos, 8–9
Minos (periodical), 87
months, 128
Moon, B., x
Mycenae, 6–7, 9, 36, 38, 73, 89, 101, 112, 119, 127, 137–8, 146

Mycenaean
    culture, 10–11, 24, 101–33
    dialect, 12, 73, 77–8, 92, 95, 131–3
    period, 7
Myres, J. L., 8, 18–19, 23, 48, 69–70

Nestor, 36, 82, 109
Nilsson, M., 87
numerals, 16, 44, 148

olive oil, 116, 126, 136, 161
Olivier, J.-P., 144, 149, 154
orthography, *see* spelling conventions
oxen, 119, 126

Palmer, L. R., x, 79, 88, 93, 112–13, 118, 152, 155
perfumes, 116, 126
personal names, 89, 92, 98, 102, 145–6, 154
Persson, A., 30–1
Peruzzi, E., 48
Phaistos, 12, 13, 91
Phaistos disk, 19–20, 27, 29–30, 156
physician, 117
pigs, 119
place-names, 31, 62, 105, 107
Platon, N., 85–6
Pleuron, 104, 138
Pope, M., 155
Poseidon, 30, 114, 124, 126
Potnia, 125–6, 156
potters, 117
Pre-Hellenic
    archaeology, 7, 10
    inhabitants of Greece, 102
    language, 31
publication of Linear B texts, 18–19, 37–8, 52, 89, 144
Pugliese Carratelli, G., 15, 19, 48
Pylos, 36–8, 104–6, 112, 133, 137, 144–5, 151

Ras Shamra (Ugarit), 21, 62, 127
Risch, E., 136
rowers, 105
Ruipérez, M. S., 84

Schachermeyr, F., 47
Schliemann, H., 6, 11, 36, 101, 146
scribes, 38, 102, 126–30, 150
Scripta Minoa I, 17; *II*, 18–19, 23, 39, 60, 62, 67

163

Index